Balancing Agility and Discipline

Balancing Agility and Discipline

A Guide for the Perplexed

Barry Boehm
Richard Turner

♦♦ Addison-Wesley

Boston • San Francisco • New York • Toronto
Montreal • London • Munich • Paris • Madrid
Capetown • Sydney • Tokyo • Singapore • Mexico City

Many of the designations used by manufacturers and sellers to distinguish their products are claimed as trademarks. Where those designations appear in this book, and Addison-Wesley was aware of a trademark claim, the designations have been printed with initial capital letters or in all capitals.

CMM, CMMI, Capability Maturity Model, Capability Maturity Modeling, and Carnegie Mellon are registered in the U.S. Patent and Trademark Office by Carnegie Mellon University.

CMM Integration; Personal Software Process; PSP; SCAMPI; Team Software Process; and TSP are service marks of Carnegie Mellon University.

Some images © 2002–2003 www.clipart.com.

The authors and publisher have taken care in the preparation of this book, but make no expressed or implied warranty of any kind and assume no responsibility for errors or omissions. No liability is assumed for incidental or consequential damages in connection with or arising out of the use of the information or programs contained herein.

The publisher offers discounts on this book when ordered in quantity for bulk purchases and special sales. For more information, please contact:

U.S. Corporate and Government Sales
(800) 382-3419
corpsales@pearsontechgroup.com

For sales outside of the U.S., please contact:

International Sales
(317) 581-3793
international@pearsontechgroup.com

Visit Addison-Wesley on the Web: www.awprofessional.com

Library of Congress Cataloging in Publication Data
Boehm, Barry
    Balancing agility and discipline : a guide for the perplexed / Barry Boehm, Richard Turner.
        p.   cm.
    Includes bibliographical references and index.
    ISBN 0-321-18612-5 (alk. paper)
    1. Computer software—Development.   I. Turner, Richard, 1954–   II. Title.

QA76.76.D47B635 2003
005.1—dc21   2003051876

Copyright © 2004 by Pearson Education, Inc.

ISBN 0-321-18612-5

Text printed in the United States on recycled paper at RR Donnelley in Crawfordsville, Indiana.

Eighth printing, February 2012

Contents

Chapter 1
Discipline, Agility, and Perplexity

Chapter 2
Contrasts and Home Grounds

Chapter 3
A Day in the Life

Chapter 4

Expanding the Home Grounds: Two Case Studies

Chapter 5
Using Risk to Balance Agility and Discipline

Chapter 6
Conclusions

Appendix A
Comparing the Methods

Appendix B
Manifesto for Agile Software Development

Appendix C
Capability Maturity Models

Appendix D
Tools for Balancing

Appendix E
Empirical Information

Foreword
by Grady Booch

There's a delightful irony in the fact that the very book you are holding in your hands has an agile pair of authors yet requires three times as many forewords as you'd find in any normal book.

Well, this is not a normal book; rather, it's a very pragmatic book that is not only quite approachable, but it is also immediately useful.

I have now personally lived through three generations of method wars. The era of structured analysis and design methods initially found its voice in methodologists such as Tom DeMarco, Ed Yourdon, Larry Constantine, Harlan Mills, Michael Jackson, and many others. There is an essential structured method that one can extract from their collective experience, but in the midst of that era, there was a veritable cacophony of competing approaches. The era of object-oriented analysis and design methods found its voice in methodologists such as Jim Rumbaugh, Ivar Jacobson, Peter Coad, Stephen Mellor, Watts Humphrey, myself, and many others. Here too one can extract some essential best practices (which is what the Rational Unified Process is all about), but still, that era was also characterized by dueling methods, each on a path to total world domination. Now we find ourselves in the post-dot-bomb era, and a fresh way of building systems has arisen, with individuals such as Kent Beck, Martin Fowler, Robert Martin, Jim Highsmith, and many others giving voice to the movement.

I expect that this won't be the last set of method wars I'll live through.

Actually, it's a sign of extreme health for our industry that there exists such a vibrant community of practice dealing with process and the developer experience. As I often quote from Bjarne Stroustrup, our civilization runs on software. Building quality software that has economic value has been, is, and will remain a hard thing to do, and thus energy spent on improving processes is energy spent on reducing the friction of software development.

Barry and Rich are in an excellent position to examine the current method wars from a dispassionate, calculating way. In this book, they extract the essential practices from the more high-ceremony methods as well as the more low-ceremony ones. Their day in the life of the developer is absolutely wonderful in highlighting the differences and similarities among methods in this spectrum of ceremony.

This day in the life work alone is worth the price of this book, but they then go on to analyze two extended case studies from the real world. As they explain in the following section, taking a risk-driven approach is a pragmatic means of reconciling the strengths and weaknesses of disciplined and agile methods.

Being a certified bibliophile and a professional geek, I have more shelf space devoted to books on software methods than any reasonable human should possess. *Balancing Agility and Discipline* has a prominent place in that section of my library, because it has helped me sort through the noise and smoke of the current method wars.

—Grady Booch
Chief Scientist
IBM Rational Software

Foreword
by Alistair Cockburn

It was brave of Barry Boehm and Rich Turner to ask me to write a foreword for their book. They risk that as a founding agilite, I'll take exception to their characterization of the agile position.

Actually, I agree with them. They manage to peer through the rhetoric to uncover the strengths and weaknesses of the agile practices and to then compare and contrast those with the strengths and weaknesses of the plan-driven practices. They go further, showing how to borrow from each when the situation calls for it. This is no small accomplishment. I commend the authors for having managed it, and for making the result readable at the same time.

A word I find interesting throughout their discussion is *discipline.* The concept of discipline runs its separate way through both the plan-driven and agile camps. My Crystal Clear methodology is as low on the discipline scale as I can make it. On the other hand, eXtreme Programming (XP) calls for high levels of discipline, as anyone who has attempted it can attest. In fact, along with Watts Humphrey's Personal Software Process (PSP), I list XP as among the highest-discipline methodologies I know. So we have both low-discipline and high-discipline examples of agile approaches, and plan-driven and agile examples of high-discipline methodologies.

In their thoughtful way, Barry and Rich capture this and inform us that plan-driven and agile approaches lean on different meanings of the word *discipline:*

> [T]he term *disciplined,* whose dictionary definition includes both "common compliance with established processes" and "self-control,"

is confined to "process compliance" by CMM bureaucrats, and confined to "self-control" by agile free spirits.

They remind us:

> If one has strong discipline without agility, the result is bureaucracy and stagnation. Agility without discipline is the unencumbered enthusiasm of a startup company before it has to turn a profit.

That is, both types of discipline are needed, in varying degrees. Part of the difference between plan-driven and agile approaches comes with highlighting one or the other meaning of the word *discipline*. Balancing your approach is much about balancing the two meanings of the word. That balancing is one of the things this book describes.

This is an outstanding book on an emotionally complicated topic. I applaud the authors for the care with which they have handled the subject.

—Alistair Cockburn
President, Humans and
Technology Project Director,
Agile Development Conference

Foreword

by Arthur Pyster

It is hard to argue against being agile and equally hard to disdain having discipline. The challenge is finding the right mix of agility and discipline. Many organizations have made great strides in productivity, predictability, quality, and cost using CMM-based process improvement—an approach that fosters disciplined processes. I have helped dozens of organizations make those strides using the Software CMM, the Systems Engineering CMM, and most recently, the CMM Integration. When properly applied, CMM-based process improvement works well. Of course, I have also seen organizations use the CMM to create stifling processes. Any tool can be misused.

For the past six years, I have worked at the Federal Aviation Administration (FAA)—the last four as Deputy Chief Information Officer. Billions of dollars are invested annually to safely move 700,000,000 passengers throughout U.S. airspace. The systems that manage air traffic share several characteristics that drive the FAA to disciplined execution of its development processes. Those systems require very high assurance and long lead times dictated by massive capital investment by government, airlines, manufacturers, and airports. System requirements are constrained by international agreements that ensure air traffic control works uniformly around the world. Air traffic control systems must be fair to all parties and must be installed while people are seven miles in the air. Careful long-range planning, stable requirements and architecture, and detailed documentation are essential to implementing and deploying such systems.

Nevertheless, processes for building air traffic systems can and do support aspects of agility. Ten years ago, air traffic control systems were built with very stilted processes. Today, spiral development, incremental development, and incremental deployment are common. Lighter-weight processes are used early in the life cycle to prototype systems, refine requirements, and evolve architectures. Stakeholders are involved early and often to ensure that requirements are valid and human interfaces are effective. I expect the FAA to continue to probe where more agile processes can reduce cost and speed deployment, while recognizing the demanding environment in which these systems must operate.

Balancing agility and discipline is essential in any sizable project. The authors have done a commendable job of identifying five critical factors—personnel, criticality, size, culture, and dynamism—for creating the right balance of flexibility and structure. Their thoughtful analysis will help developers who must sort through the agile-discipline debate, giving them guidance to create the right mix for their projects.

—Arthur Pyster
Deputy Assistant Administrator
for Information Services and
Deputy Chief Information Officer
Federal Aviation Administration

Preface

Why We Wrote This Book

In the last few years, two ostensibly conflicting approaches to software development have competed for hegemony. Agile method supporters released a manifesto that shifts the focus from traditional plan-driven, process-based methods to lighter, more adaptive paradigms. Traditional methods have reasserted the need for strong process discipline and rigorous practices. True believers on both sides have raised strident, often antagonistic, voices.

True believers represent software development alternatives

We wrote this book for the rest of us—those caught in the middle of the method wars, simply trying to get our projects completed and accepted within too-tight schedules and budgets. We hope to clarify the perplexity about the roles of discipline, agility, and process in software development. We objectively compare and contrast the traditional, plan-driven approaches to the newer agile approaches and present an overview of their home grounds, strengths, and weaknesses. We then describe a risk-based approach to aid in balancing agility and discipline within a software development project.

This book is for the rest of us

We hope that this is a practical book. It is intended to be neither academic nor exhaustive, but pragmatic. It is based on our own development experiences, current and past literature, long conversations with proponents of agile and plan-driven approaches, teaching students how to balance discipline and agility, and years of observing and measuring software development in industry, government, and academia. We discuss the subject matter absent a need to choose sides. Our goal is to help you gain the understanding and information you need to integrate the approaches in a manner that best fits your business environment.

Our goal is to help you in your business environment

Who Should Read This Book

The perplexed—
or just curious

This book is for perplexed software and management professionals who have heard the buzz about agile methods and want to separate the chaff from the wheat. Perhaps you have a CMM- or ISO-certified organization and want to know if and how agile methods can help you. Or perhaps some part of your organization has adopted agile methods and you are unsure of how they should fit in. Fundamentally, if you need to understand how the latest software development approaches can help meet business goals, this book is for you.

- *Software project managers and mid-level executives* should read this book to understand the agile/plan-driven controversy and learn how best to apply the new approaches in your organizations.
- *Software developers* should read this book to better understand how your field is evolving and what it means for your career.
- *Computer science and software engineering students* should read this book to better understand how to make choices about your own balance of agility and discipline, both in school and at work.
- *Academicians* should read this book to understand some of what your students are asking about, and how to help them make informed decisions.
- *Proponents of both agile and plan-driven methods* should read this book to dispassionately look at your opponent's ideas.
- *CIOs and CEOs* should read this book to help you understand what's going on in the software world and what implications it may have for your company.

How to Read This Book

Several ways to
read the book

Most of you are busy people, and "must-read" material attacks you from all sides, 24/7. Some of you want to quickly assess the material for later reflection. Others want to know how to implement the concepts we present. For that reason, we've tried to make this book easy to read quickly but with pointers to more in-depth material.

To support the various reading needs, we've reused a format success-fully employed by David Taylor in his outstanding *Object Technology: A Manager's Guide.* The margins contain a "fast track" summary of the text. We've included illustrations for key concepts. We've also included sidebar material that amplifies the text.

Margin summaries for fast track reading

In order to meet the needs of the broadest possible audience, we have written the main text to provide basic information and relegated much of the technical material to appendices. Because of the authors' empirical backgrounds, one appendix covers the latest in empirical studies related to agility and discipline. The following icons will appear to indicate that additional material on the current topic is available in the appendices:

More information in the appendices

✘ Information on tools and techniques (Appendix D)

⊞ Empirical material (Appendix E)

If time is short, use the fast track summaries to scan the total content of the book, stopping to read things you find interesting or particularly applicable to your needs, and following the icons for specific technical information. If you find you need even more detailed material, see the References section for a list of additional resources.

In a hurry? Use the fast track for a quick overview

You can also tailor your reading through chapter selection. Reading the first and last chapters gives a pretty good idea of the material at a famil-iarization level. You can read the chapters in any order. Here is a quick summary:

First and last chapters are key

Chapter 1 sets the stage for what follows. It introduces the main points and provides an executive summary of the book.

Chapter 2 compares the agile and plan-driven approaches and provides insight into the type of projects where each has been most successful—their home grounds.

Chapter 3 provides an experiential introduction to the approaches by describing how both a typical and not-so-typical day might be spent using each approach.

Chapter 4 presents two project case studies that illustrate the limits of pure agile and pure plan-driven implementations and the benefits of integrating the approaches.

Chapter 5 describes a risk-based approach for making methodology decisions that integrate agile and plan-driven practices, and illustrates it with representative examples.

Chapter 6 summarizes the material and offers some final observations.

Appendix A provides top-level descriptions of the major agile and plan-driven methods, highlighting their primary distinguishing factors, and a summary of those factors for comparison.

Appendices B through E provide technical and background information to support our analyses and speak to specific technical topics.

The Notes (listed by chapter) and the References follow Appendix E.

Acknowledgments

It is hard to know where to begin thanking the many people involved with creating this book. First there are the three foreword authors, who also reviewed the book draft and identified key improvements: Grady Booch, Alistair Cockburn, and Arthur Pyster. We were also fortunate to have a broad spectrum of reviewers of the full book draft whose perspectives provided many insightful improvement suggestions: Pekka Abrahamsson, Kristen Baldwin, Marguerite Brown, Scott Duncan, Peter Hantos, Denise Howard, Tony Jordano, Mikael Lindvall, Ken Schwaber, and Laurie Williams.

We would also like to thank very much those busy leaders in the agile and plan-driven communities who shared their time and expertise in helping us to see the software world from many different points of view: Scott Ambler, Ken Auer, Vic Basili, Kent Beck, Larry Bernstein, Winsor Brown, Bob Charette, Steve Cross, Michael Crowley, Christine Davis, Noopur Davis, Tom DeMarco, Nancy Eickelmann, Amr Elssamadisy, Hakan Erdogmus, Mike Falat, Martin Fowler, James Grenning, Jim Highsmith, Tom Hilburn, George Huling, Tuomo Kahkonen, Bil Kleb, William Krebs, Philippe Kruchten, Charles Leinbach, Wei Li, John Manzo, Frank Maurer, Granville Miller, Karen Owens, Mark Paulk, Gary Pollice, Dan Port, Don Reifer, Walker Royce, Gregory Schalliol, Kurt Schneider, Sarah Sheard, Giancarlo Succi, Roland Trauter, David Webb, Christian Wege, Laurie Williams, and William Wood. As the views of the people listed above differ considerably and we have tried to respect their views, our listing them does not imply that they agree with everything in the book.

We are especially grateful to our CeBASE colleagues—Mohammed Al-Said, LiGuo Huang, Apurva Jain, LaDonna Pierce, Meghna Shah,

Sachin Shah, Gunjan Sharman, and Paul Sitko from the University of Southern California Center for Software Engineering, and Patricia Costa, Atif Memon, Forrest Shull, Roseanne Tesoriero Tvedt, and Marv Zelkowitz from the Fraunhofer Center at the University of Maryland—for their support in the research of agile and plan-driven methods, particularly through the e-Workshops and the two agile methods workshops held at USC. Peter Gordon and the Addison-Wesley staff were, as always, excellent partners.

Finally, we offer love and thanks to our wives—Sharla and Jo—who not only put up with midnight faxes, travel extensions, and the general absent-mindedness that go with this kind of project, but also provided perceptive reviews and editorial suggestions that improved the book immensely. As always, they are our best inspiration and most honest critics, and we love them for both.

Prelude

Once upon a time, in a land steeped in metaphor, there lived an elephant. For many years, this reliable elephant served his village as the principal food gatherer and knew just what the village needed. He established paths through the jungle that always led him to the best roots, vegetables, nuts, and fruits. He knew which fruits he could reach with his trunk and which ones required some trunk shaking. His massive strength enabled him to bring back enough food for several days, so he always anticipated the requirements of the village and maintained adequate supplies. He was faithful to his task, was appreciated throughout the village, and thought his life most rewarding.

Alas, things began to change, as they often do in life and fable. The village cooks wanted different, rarer ingredients for their cooking, things the elephant had heard of but were not along his well-worn trail. He busily maintained stores of food that no one wanted but couldn't find time to make new paths for meeting new requests. The village grew impatient with the discouraged elephant, who just couldn't keep up with the demands.

Around the same time, there was a monkey in a nearby village whose job mirrored that of the elephant. Unlike the elephant, however, the agile monkey flitted across the jungle grabbing fruit as he saw it, finding the low-hanging fruit and bringing it quickly back to the village cooks. Rather than the time-proven trails of the elephant, the monkey relied on his memory and instincts

to find food and brought back only the amount needed that day. Sometimes he ran off looking for increasingly exotic foods and occasionally got lost. But his speed and agility always proved equal to the tasks the village set for him, and like the elephant, he was greatly appreciated.

Unfortunately, the monkey's life changed, too. His successful village grew larger every day. The monkey had so many requests that he was constantly on the move, trying to remember all the needs at every location. He had to make many more trips because he just didn't have the strength to carry everything requested at the same time. The village began to get impatient with him as well, and the monkey began to doubt he could do the job.

As luck would have it, the weary monkey and the discouraged elephant met one day. The monkey, trying to move quickly with a large load, noticed how much food the elephant was carrying in the panniers on his back. The elephant was impressed with the monkey's speed, how far he could travel, and how easily he could gather some of the food that the elephant struggled to reach. Both animals, proud of their skills, nevertheless acknowledged that there were obvious advantages to the other's abilities.

The elephant and monkey recognized the benefits of working together and decided to join forces. The monkey would use his agility to meet the new requests to find distant fruit, bringing it back to the elephant for his village. The elephant would carry sufficient quantities of food to the monkey's village to meet the growing needs of the population. It took them a while to work out just how to do this, but soon they had things going well for both villages. And so, they lived happily ever after, secure in their mutual trust and the appreciation of well-fed villagers.

1

Discipline, Agility, and Perplexity

Perplexity abounds about agility, discipline, and software development

Discipline is the foundation for any successful endeavor. Athletes train, musicians practice, craftsmen perfect techniques, and engineers apply processes. Without these basic skills there may be an occasional success using natural talent, but professional consistency and long-term prospects are limited. The strength and comfort that come from discipline support the endeavor when things are difficult, when the body or mind is under the weather, or when something new or unexpected arises and a response is required. Discipline creates well-organized memories, history, and experience.

Discipline provides strength and comfort

Agility is the counterpart of discipline. Where discipline ingrains and strengthens, agility releases and invents. It allows athletes to make the unexpected play, musicians to improvise and ornament, craftsmen to evolve their style, and engineers to adjust to changing technology and needs. Agility applies memory and history to adjust to new environments,

Agility releases and invents

react and adapt, take advantage of unexpected opportunities, and update the experience base for the future.

Successful projects need both

As our friends in the Prelude discovered, every successful venture in a changing world requires both agility and discipline. This is as true in business and software development as it is in sports and art. In his best-seller *Good to Great,* Jim Collins presents a two-dimensional scale that describes the characteristics of successful businesses. One dimension is discipline and the other, entrepreneurial attitude, or in our context, agility. If one has strong discipline without agility, the result is bureaucracy and stagnation. Agility without discipline is the unencumbered enthusiasm of a startup company before it has to turn a profit. Great companies have both in measures appropriate to their goals and environment.

The software environment is changing

The environment in which software is imagined, specified, and created is changing. Software systems are becoming much larger and more complex, commercial-off-the-shelf components are playing more significant roles, and the rapid pace of requirements changes is accelerating. Software has become ubiquitous, making its quality and usability aspects more critical. Time-to-market can spell the difference between a successful product release and bankruptcy.

Traditional development focuses on plans and architectures

The traditional software development world, characterized by the engineering and process improvement advocates, has addressed this changing environment by relying on foresight to develop and enforce architectures that can often tame change before it adversely impacts the system. Their plan-driven methods focus on the quality of the software artifacts and the predictability of their processes.

Traditional approaches are best exemplified by the Capability Maturity Model for Software (SW-CMM),[1] which gained prominence in the late

1980s and early 1990s. The SW-CMM is based on the quality work of Crosby,[2] Deming,[3] and Juran[4], is related to software work of Humphrey,[5] and is informed by considerable experience with highly disciplined software processes in aerospace and commercial industries. It provides a road map of activities and practices to guide an organization through five levels of software process maturity:

CMM exemplifies traditional, plan-driven approach

- Ad hoc, chaotic
- Repeatable
- Defined
- Managed
- Optimizing

SW-CMM has been revised and augmented by the release of the Capability Maturity Model Integration (CMMI) products.[6, 7] CMMI places software process in the larger context of systems engineering.

Thousands of organizations have embraced the SW-CMM and have found that their software development became less chaotic. But many organizations, including some of the SW-CMM adopters, were perplexed about various costs of using it: "It feels like we're spending more time writing documents than producing software. Can't we get along with less?" Or, "The world is changing so fast, it seems like there's a cost of trying to be repeatable or too optimized. That's what the dinosaurs were, and where are they now?"

SW-CMM has a large community of users—some with questions

In the last few years, the mainstream software development community has been challenged by a counter-culture movement that addresses change from a radically different perspective. This new approach, called "agile" by its proponents, is best exemplified by their Agile Manifesto:[8]

Agile methods represent a different perspective

> We have come to value
>> Individuals and interactions over process and tools
>> Working software over comprehensive documentation
>> Customer collaboration over contract negotiation
>> Responding to change over following a plan.
>> That is, while there is value in the items on the right, we value the items on the left more.

Agile methods lighten process

Agile methods encourage programmers to shed their heavyweight process chains, embrace change, and escape into agility. Advocated methods have short cycle times, close customer involvement, and an adaptive rather than predictive mind set.

Agile methods are being widely adopted—with questions

An increasing number of organizations have embraced one or more of the agile methods, producing software with less documentation under conditions of rapid change to the high satisfaction of clients. But here again, many organizations are perplexed about the risks involved in those preferences: "Can you do big projects without comprehensive documentation?" "If we just spent six months getting a dozen stakeholders to agree to a plan, should we scrap it every time one of them wants a change?"

The approaches have become adversarial

Unfortunately, rather than find ways to support each other, these two approaches to software development have considered each other opponents in a zero-sum game. The agilists rail against the traditionalists and lament the dehumanization of software development by "Taylorian" reductionists who worship process. The establishment has responded with accusations of hacking, poor quality, and having way too much fun in a serious business. True believers on both sides have emerged to proclaim their convictions with near-messianic stridency, raising the perplexity level of software developers and managers trying to evolve their success strategies.

At this bumper-sticker level, there are clearly ways to misinterpret the approaches and many things to be perplexed about. To further complicate matters, both of the approaches are evolving, moving targets. In this book we will look carefully at each approach. We will try to draw distinctions between them, identify the conditions under which they appear to work best, and show how the best of each can be combined into hybrid approaches.

A balanced approach is possible

The Sources of Perplexity

Over and above the seemingly opposing viewpoints of the two approaches, there are a number of other sources of perplexity that complicate the search for understanding. These are not diabolical, but stem from strong opinions, genuine misunderstandings, and perhaps some marketing hyperbole. In this section we'll examine a few of those sources that this book tries to explain.

Strong opinions, misunderstanding, and marketing contribute to complexity

Multiple Definitions

Probably the easiest source of perplexity to identify, and perhaps the most difficult to resolve, is that of multiple definitions for the same word. For example, the term *disciplined,* whose dictionary definition includes both "common compliance with established processes" and "self-control," is confined to process compliance by CMM bureaucrats, and confined to self-control by agile free spirits. Similarly, *agility* has been selectively interpreted positively as "dexterity" and negatively as "inconstancy of purpose."

The same word can mean different things

A further example is *quality.* In the SW-CMM, "quality assurance" is defined as "specification and process compliance." Agile methods see quality as essentially customer satisfaction.

Quality: customer satisfaction or compliance?

Distinguishing Method Use from Method Misuse

Sometimes negative examples stem from misuse

Some perplexity arises when examples of method use are in fact examples of method misuse. We've all heard comments about agile being equated with hacking, but an example shows that such negative comments can have a root in misapplication.

"eXtreme Programming is hacking" example

Here is an example of agile misuse:

> eXtreme Programming expert Bob Martin said at the 2001 XP Universe conference that he ran into someone who said his organization was using XP. Martin asked him how the pair programming was viewed, and the reply was, "We don't do that." Martin asked how refactoring was working out, and the reply was, "We don't do that." Martin asked how well the planning game was working, and the reply was, "We don't do that." "Well," Martin asked, "then what are you doing?" "We don't document anything!" was the answer.[9]

"Plan-driven methods need too much documentation" example

In other situations, the misuse results from a need to satisfy criteria other than good project performance. An excellent example of overdisciplined bureaucracy was a picture of the "CMM Level 4 Memorial Library" recently exhibited by an aerospace company. It showed bookcase upon bookcase of 99 2-inch binders containing evidence of SW-CMM Level 4 process compliance. These were not produced to help the project, but to pass an external appraisal required to obtain an authorized CMM Level 4 rating.

Overgeneralization Based on the Most Visible Instances

Only hear the loudest voices

A third source of perplexity is the tendency to consider the most visible (or vocal) examples of a methodology as representative of the entire family.

XP doesn't reflect the entire agile community

Agile methods are often equated with eXtreme Programming (XP) because it is the most visible example. True to its name, XP prescribes quite extreme interpretations of good practices in ways that do not accurately represent the entire agile community.

A similar occurrence in the traditional world is the equating of discipline with the SW-CMM. Certainly a CMM can help add discipline to an organization, but it is primarily a set of criteria and a map for process improvement—not a software development approach. For example, the SW-CMM doesn't address personnel issues—they are covered in a separate model, the People CMM. Besides, there are other ways of instilling order (product standards, formal methods) outside the process improvement milieu.

CMM is not the only source of order

Claims of Universality

It is easy to assume universality when we find something that works. This is the essence of a silver bullet, whose life cycle has been delightfully described by Sarah Sheard of the Software Productivity Consortium as a journey through discovery, successful application, publicity of success, momentum building and publication, first (slightly modified) replication, confirmation by early adopters, proceduralization and implementation in disparate environments by uninformed middle management, insufficient funding and misapplication, diminishing returns due to devolution of original idea, denigration of the original idea, and ultimately demise and new discovery.[10]

One size fits all is a myth

In the agile world, the claim often takes the form of a syllogism assumed (but certainly not proven) as follows: The pace of information technology (IT) change is accelerating *and* agile methods adapt to change better than disciplined methods *therefore* agile methods will take over the IT world. A parallel plan-driven version might be: Software development is uncertain *and* the SW-CMM improves predictability *therefore* all software developers should use the SW-CMM.

Both agile and plan-driven proponents are guilty

Early Success Stories

Early success doesn't always mean longevity

Another source of perplexity is the difficulty of calibrating the unabashed joy and enthusiasm accompanying early successes without data about the staying power of new methods. For example, in the agile world, the initially successful Chrysler Comprehensive Compensation (C3) project that gave birth to XP as a remedy for failed traditional methods was eventually cancelled. Cleanroom, one of the most successful and empirically studied of the formal, process-based methods, has never really crossed Moore's chasm into the mainstream.

Purist Interpretations

"Only one way to implement" is misleading

Finally, there is the "fish versus fowl" purity of practice issue. Must one implement the approach exactly and in its entirety, or can the practitioner make value judgments on what meets their needs? Or, more simply, is it valid to be a partial or hybrid implementer?

Two quotes from agilists illustrate disagreement within the agile ranks:

- "Don't start by incrementally adopting parts of XP. Its pieces fit together like a fine Swiss watch."
- "An advantage of agile methods is that you can apply them selectively and generatively."

The plan-driven world is similarly divided, as exemplified by these statements:

- "If you aren't 100 percent compliant with SW-CMM Level 3, don't bother to bid."
- "With the CMMI continuous interpretation, you can improve your processes in any order you feel is best."

Clarifying Perplexity

It is our intent to clarify and explain the roots of most of the sources of perplexity. We will start off with a quick introduction to the two approaches and move rapidly into describing the differences, providing examples of pure and mixed application, and developing a way to use risk to balance agile and plan-driven methods in a software project.

We'll examine the roots of perplexity and ways to conquer it

The Two Approaches

It is important to understand the character and background of agile and plan-driven methods to truly appreciate the controversy. In this section, we discuss the two methods independently and then compare their significant differences as well as their obvious similarities.

Knowledge about both approaches is necessary for evaluation

As discussed in our litany of perplexity sources, definitions are always tricky. This is generally because of the "loading" of certain commonly used words with narrow, methodology-specific meanings. In the case of agile and plan-driven methods, this is made more complicated by the number of different methods and the wide variety of vocabulary.

Some difficulties with definitions

Plan-Driven Methods

Plan-driven methods are generally considered the traditional way to develop software. Based on concepts drawn from the mainline engineering fields, these methods approach development in a requirements/design/build paradigm with standard, well-defined processes that organizations improve continuously.

The "traditional" way to develop software

The genesis of plan-driven approaches lies in the systems engineering and quality disciplines. During the rise of the big aerospace systems—satellites, manned spacecraft, ballistic missiles—the tenets of systems engineering were established to coordinate large numbers of precisely

Based on engineering disciplines and large aerospace development

interoperating components not necessarily produced by a single company or group of workers.

Software proved difficult to manage

While hardware components seemed to fit nicely into this paradigm, software was not as well understood and didn't have the inherent physical constraints of hardware. Generally, there was a very undisciplined approach to software development that did not merge well into the "systems" arena. The result was software that was more often than not late, over budget, and of low quality.

Standards were introduced

To counter this, the U.S. Department of Defense (DoD) began to develop a series of guidance documents that provided instructions for making the software development process fit the systems approach. These documents are best represented by MIL-STD-1521, DoD-STD-2167, MIL-STD-498, and their successors. At the same time, large commercial companies, including IBM, Hitachi, and Siemens, developed similar standards for their internal use.

Process discipline and structured techniques were developed

So, as software engineering became more important, methods for "disciplining" the development of software began to appear. In order to integrate easily into the overall system development environment, these methods reflected the needs and approaches of the existing engineering processes. They also fitted well with the branch of academic computer science and software engineering that views software development as a process of formal mathematical specification and verification.

Characteristics

Value well-defined work products, verification, and validation

Plan-driven methods are characterized by a systematic engineering approach to software that carefully adheres to specific processes in moving software through a series of representations from requirements to finished code. There is a concern for completeness of documentation at every step of the way so that thorough verification of each representation may be accomplished after the fact. The original tendency was to view the development cycle as a waterfall from the concept through to the end product. More recently, incremental and evolutionary processes have been adopted, but still with strong documentation and traceability mandates across requirements, design, and code.

The malleability of software as a product makes it necessary to support these multiple versions of product definition with process. The definition and management of processes is key to plan-driven methods. For that reason, plan-driven methods are almost always associated with process improvement. The processes need to be defined, standardized, and incrementally improved to provide the data needed to control and manage their operation. Such processes generally include detailed plans, activities, workflow, roles and responsibilities, and work product descriptions. The people who perform them must be trained in their application, and there is often a group of individuals who act as the process monitoring, controlling, and educating infrastructure. Figure 1-1 illustrates an example of process management.

Product discipline is equally coupled with process definition and improvement

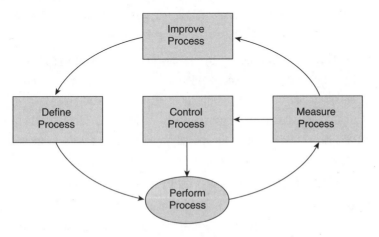

Figure 1-1   A Process Improvement Cycle

Provide predictability and mitigate turnover through repeatability and infrastructure

The strengths of plan-driven methods are in the comparability and repeatability that standardization brings. By defining the way specific processes are performed and specific work products are formatted, any person trained in the organizational process will know where to look for information and how to go about estimating common work. The amount of information maintained within the process means that managers can move personnel quickly between projects (or subprojects) without a great deal of retraining, and that a loss of key personnel will not necessarily doom a project.

Some Important Plan-Driven Concepts

Process improvement   A program of activities designed to improve the performance and maturity of the organization's processes, and the results of such a program. Process improvement grew out of the quality management work of Deming, Crosby, and Juran and is aimed at increasing the capability of work processes.

Process capability   The inherent ability of a process to produce planned results. As the capability of each process is improved, it becomes predictable and measurable, and the most significant causes of poor quality and productivity are controlled or eliminated. This narrows the range of expected and actual results that can be achieved by following a process.

Organizational maturity   By steadily improving its process capability, an organization is said to mature. Maturity encompasses not only individual project capability, but the common application of standard processes across an organization. Common processes are maintained and personnel trained in their application. Projects tailor the common process assets to meet their needs. Once common assets are deployed, the organization can begin to measure their effectiveness and improve them based on the measures.

Process group   A collection of specialists that facilitate the definition, maintenance, and improvement of the process(es) used by an organization.

Process groups may address software engineering processes only (SEPG) or engineering processes (EPG).

Risk management An organized, analytic process to identify uncertainties that might cause harm or loss (identify risks), assess and quantify the identified risks, and develop and apply risk management plans to prevent or handle risk causes that could result in significant harm or loss.

Verification Verification confirms that work products (e.g., specifications, designs, models) properly reflect the requirements specified for them (building the product right).

Validation Validation confirms the fitness or worth of a work product for its operational mission (building the right product).

Software system architecture A software system architecture defines a collection of software and system components, connectors, and constraints; a collection of system stakeholders' need statements; and a rationale which demonstrates that the components, connectors, and constraints define a system that, if implemented, would satisfy the collection of system stakeholders' need statements.

Of course, planning can also cause problems. If too strictly applied, plans and process can impede innovation or lead to a mechanical, checklist mentality, where the object of the endeavor becomes so focused on the process that the product (often along with the customer) is afforded secondary status. People caught up in heavy process also run the risk of becoming documentation generators instead of software developers.

Planning can become mechanistic and succumb to a checklist mentality

Requirements for Success

Plan-driven methods require management support, organizational infrastructure, and an environment where practitioners understand the importance of common processes to their personal work and the success of the enterprise. Management must understand that processes are vital to

Management support and infrastructure are key

the delivery of the product, and that circumventing them can add significant cost and schedule risk. The infrastructure for plan-driven processes includes process asset libraries that encourage process reuse, process training for practitioners, and usually a process management staff that supports the maintenance of process documentation.

Examples of Plan-Driven Approaches

Method	Players	Description
Military standards	DoD	DoD-STD-2167 was a document-driven approach that specified a large number of Data Item Descriptions for deliverables. Tailoring was encouraged, but was rarely effectively done. MIL-STD-1521 details a set of sequential reviews and audits required. MIL-STD-498 revised 2167 to allow more flexibility in systems engineering, planning, development, and integration. MIL-STD-499B defines the contents of a systems engineering management plan.
General process standards	ISO, EIA, IEEE	EIA/IEEE J-STD-016 was a generallization of MIL-STD-498 to include commercial software processes. ISO 9000 is a quality management standard that includes software. ISO 12207 and 15504 address the software life cycle and ways to appraise software processes.
Software factories	Hitachi, General Electric, others	A long-term, integrated effort to improve software quality, software reuse, and software development productivity. Highly process-driven, emphasizing early defect reduction.

Method	Players	Description
Cleanroom	Harlan Mills, IBM	Uses statistical process control and mathematically based verification to develop software with certified reliability. The name "Cleanroom" comes from physical clean rooms that prevent defects in precision electronics.
Capability Maturity Model Software (SW-CMM)	SEI, Air Force, Watts Humphrey, Mark Paulk	A process improvement framework, SW-CMM grew out of the need for the Air Force to select qualified software system developers. Collects best practices into Key Practice Areas that are organized into five levels of increasing process maturity.
CMM Integration (CMMI)	SEI, DoD, NDIA, Roger Bate, Jack Ferguson, Mike Phillips	CMMI was established by DoD and the National Defense Industrial Association (NDIA) to integrate software and systems engineering CMMs, and improve or extend the CMM concept to other disciplines. CMMI is a suite of models and appraisal methods that address a variety of disciplines using a common architecture, vocabulary, and core of process areas.
Personal Software Process (PSP) / Team Software Process (TSP)	Watts Humphrey, SEI	PSP is a structured framework of forms, guidelines, and procedures for developing software. It is directed toward the use of self-measurement to improve individual programming skills. TSP builds on PSP and supports the development of industrial-strength software through the use of team planning and control.

Practitioners must be trained and supportive of the processes

Processes cannot work without the active support of the participants. Practitioners must be well trained in both the practice and philosophy of the plan-driven approach. Just like management, they must realize that the process should be given a certain amount of allegiance or else the entire strategy may fail. Some amount of individualism must be forfeited in the maintenance of a prescribed process, but often creativity must be used in adapting the process to the vagaries of the project as it progresses.

Agile Methods

Grew from rapid prototyping and a resurgence of programming as a craft

Agile methods are an outgrowth of rapid prototyping and rapid development experiences as well as the resurgence of the philosophy that programming is a craft rather than an industrial process. There is a strong undercurrent of disdain for the mechanical, often seen as dehumanizing, application of plan-driven software development.

Rapid change and long development cycles don't mix

The rapidly changing nature of the Internet-based economy demands flexibility and speed from software developers, something not usually associated with plan-driven development. The problem of change is exacerbated by long development cycles that yield code that may be well written but does not meet user expectations.

Chaordic = chaos + order

The term "chaordic" has been coined for work that unifies chaos and order in a way that defies management by normal, traditional, linear planning and processes.[11] Agile methods target this chaordic work.

The Agile Manifesto defines philosophy of agility

The aforementioned Agile Manifesto is a document developed and signed by a group of agile proponents known as the Agile Alliance. The four values have been further defined by twelve principles (see Appendix B). It is important to note that the manifesto values are relative statements, not absolutes. That is, they represent a weighting of alternatives rather than a binary choice. One proponent classifies agile values as "would-be"—that is, they represent an attitude, goal, or philosophy as much as a state of accomplishment.[12]

Characteristics

In general, agile methods are very lightweight processes that employ short iterative cycles; actively involve users to establish, prioritize, and verify requirements; and rely on tacit knowledge within a team as opposed to documentation. A truly agile method must include all of the following attributes: iterative (several cycles), incremental (not deliver the entire product at once), self-organizing (teams determine the best way to handle work), and emergence (processes, principles, work structures are recognized during the project rather than predetermined). Anything less is a "lightened defined process,"[13] although such processes can exhibit considerable agility. Figure 1-2 shows an example of an agile process flow.

Lightweight processes, short iterations, and reliance on tacit knowledge

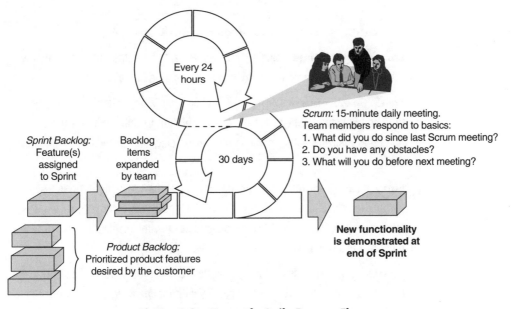

Scrum: 15-minute daily meeting. Team members respond to basics:
1. What did you do since last Scrum meeting?
2. Do you have any obstacles?
3. What will you do before next meeting?

Sprint Backlog: Feature(s) assigned to Sprint

Backlog items expanded by team

Every 24 hours

30 days

New functionality is demonstrated at end of Sprint

Product Backlog: Prioritized product features desired by the customer

**Figure 1-2   Example Agile Process Flow
(Scrum—Source: ControlChaos.com)**

Agile practices support the agile manifesto

The practices espoused to support these values, several of which are described in the accompanying sidebar, vary with the method. They can be generally classified as belonging to three general areas:

- Communication (e.g., metaphor, pair-programming)
- Management (e.g., planning game, fast cycle/frequent delivery)
- Technical (e.g., simple design, refactoring, test-driven design)

Agile practices aren't really new—mostly a new attitude and better packaging

Many of these practices have long histories (pair programming was used by Fred Brooks in the mid-1950s[14]) and should be familiar to both process improvement advocates and software engineers. The key is that they are applied in mutually reinforcing ways to the development cycle. Agilists speak of a "mentality of sufficiency"—doing only what is necessary.[15] "Barely sufficient" is another term used to denote this sparse attitude toward process.[16]

Some Important Agile Concepts

Embracing change   Seeing change as an ally rather than an enemy. Change allows for more creativity and quicker value to the customer.

Fast cycle/frequent delivery   Scheduling many releases with short time spans between them; forces implementation of only the highest priority functions, delivers value to the customer quickly, and speeds requirements emergence.

Simple design   Designing for the battle, not the war. The motto is YAGNI ("You Aren't Going to Need It"). Strips designs down to cover just what is currently being developed. Since change is inevitable, planning for future functions is a waste of effort.

Refactoring   The restructuring of software to remove duplication, improve communication, simplify, or add flexibility without changing its behavior. Just-in-time redesign.

Pair programming   A style of programming in which two programmers work side by side at one computer, continually collaborating on the same design, algorithm, code, or test.

Retrospective   A post-iteration review of the effectiveness of the work performed, methods used, and estimates. The review supports team learning and estimation for future iterations. Sometimes called "reflection."

Tacit knowledge   Agility is achieved by establishing and updating project knowledge in the participants' heads rather than in documents (explicit knowledge).

Test-driven development   Module or method tests are incrementally written by the developers and customers before and during coding. Supports and encourages very short iteration cycles.

Another goal of agile methods is to "embrace change." If change is a given, as it is in most development projects, then use techniques that take advantage of change. If requirements change rapidly, have short iterations and only do the minimum necessary to meet the current requirement set. Constantly integrate and regression test. Keep the customer close and involve them in the planning and validation processes. Redesign when needed, but don't overdesign—you probably won't need the extra hooks, since the project will most likely take a hard left before you reach the intersection you predesigned for. Don't develop documentation that becomes "shelfware" before it is bound. Concentrate totally on the current iteration and deliver a product on time that "delights the customer."[17]

Embrace change rather than fight it

Requirements for Success

Agile methods universally need close relationships with the customer and users of the systems under development. Requirements and validation are dependent on the customers' describing, prioritizing, and refining their

Close relationship with the customer is critical

needs throughout the development. The cycle of building functionality, obtaining feedback, and evolving the system based on that feedback is highly dependent on an informed and involved customer. The customer also establishes acceptance criteria and tests.

Tacit knowledge maintained within a well-qualified team

Agile methods require a critical mass of highly motivated, knowledgeable team members. Since documentation and design are kept to a minimum, the ability for team members to retain and act on tacit knowledge is crucial.

Agility often requires cultural change

Cultural acceptance of the agile rationale is also necessary to initiate and grow agility. For example, pair programming requires practitioner comfort and acceptance of working closely with another developer. It also depends on management acceptance that two people working together can be more productive and adapt more rapidly than two working alone.

Scalability is a challenge

There is considerable skepticism that pure agile methods can be used effectively with large, complex, or safety-critical software systems. Agile methods seem to be best suited for smaller programs. Although there have been large projects documented, the large majority of experience is in relatively small (5- to 10-person) projects. As we will see in Chapter 4, experience on 50-person agile projects indicates that plan-driven process aspects need to be integrated to be successful with larger projects.

Continuous improvement is integral

In the same manner as shown in Figure 1-1, the agile retrospectives and reflections enable continuous process and technical improvement. This can be a challenge, since most information in agile approaches is not documented, is maintained in the developers' mental experience base, and so is more difficult to analyze systematically.

Examples of Agile Methods

Method	Players	Description
eXtreme Programming (XP)	Kent Beck, Ward Cunningham, Ron Jeffries, Daimler Chrysler	Probably the most famous agile method. Refined from experience gained developing an information system for Daimler Chrysler Corporation. XP is fairly rigorous and initially expects all of the practices defined in the method to be followed. These practices include stories, pair programming, simple design, test first, and continuous integration.
Adaptive Software Development (ASD)	Jim Highsmith	Responding to industry turbulence and the need for rapid business development, ASD provides a philosophical base and practical approach using iterative development, feature-based planning, and customer focus group reviews within a leadership-collaboration management style.
Crystal	Alistair Cockburn	A family of methods that provide different levels of "ceremony" depending on the size of the team and the criticality of the project. Practices draw from agile and plan-driven methods as well as psychology and organizational development research.
Scrum	Ken Schwaber, Jeff Sutherland, Mike Beedle	More a management technique, Scrum projects are divided into 30-day work intervals in which a specific number of requirements from a prioritized list (backlog) are implemented. Daily 15-minute "Scrum meetings" maintain coordination.

(continued)

Examples of Agile Methods (*continued*)

Method	Players	Description
Feature-Driven Development (FDD)	Jeff DeLuca, Peter Coad	A very lightweight architecturally based process that initially establishes an overall object architecture and features list. It then proceeds to design-by-feature and build-by-feature. Maintains Chief Architect and Chief Programmer roles. The use of UML or other object-oriented design methods is strongly implied.

Finding Middle Ground

Taking a pragmatic stand among the true believers

The software world, and perhaps the world in general, is largely populated by true believers, agnostics, and pragmatists. We would like to stand as pragmatists and provide empirical guidance to the majority of managers and practitioners who are not sure they want to become single-method true believers but don't want to be disadvantaged in their agnosticism.

Both approaches have home grounds

Each of the approaches is most comfortable in what we can term as their "home ground." For plan-driven methods, that ground is generally large, complex systems, often with safety-critical or other high-reliability attributes. Requirements should be fairly stable and the environment somewhat predictable. Agile methods are more comfortable where the systems and development teams are smaller, the customer and users are readily available, and the requirements and environment are volatile.

We believe there is a middle ground

Real-world examples argue both for and against agile methods. Responding to change is a critical success factor in many time-critical projects and was cited as a driver in the Netscape-Microsoft browser wars.[18] On the other hand, over-responding to change was one of the identified causes for the $3 billion overrun of the U.S. Federal Aviation Administration's Advanced Automation System for national air traffic control.[19] We believe that common sense dictates the evaluation of both approaches for incorporation within the project manager's technical and managerial toolbox.

We stated at the beginning of this chapter that successful, sustainable software development requires both discipline and agility. Developing software in the real world involves gracefully adapting to change and handling a wide variety of environments and requirements. Consider the very different characteristics of software developed for an electronic toaster and software developed for the International Space Station.

Different mixes of discipline and agility are needed

As technology changes rapidly and customers react in Internet time for many of their products, traditional development environments must react more quickly to change and agility will become more and more important in successful development projects. Defense and other large systems must find ways to enable their methodologies to incorporate agility in order to maintain relevancy and meet their customer's needs and expectations. But the necessity of discipline to ground adaptability is as necessary as it has ever been, especially as software system size and complexity grow.

The speed of change demands agility

Rational's Philippe Kruchten has likened the CMM for Software to a dictionary; that is, one uses the words one needs to make the desired point—there is no need to use all the words available.[20] We believe that an organization should have a repository of "plug-compatible" process assets that can be quickly adopted, arranged, and put in place to support specific projects. Finding the right amount of rigor or process is a management issue that should consider the team members and their

Processes should be the right weight for the specific project, team, and environment

capabilities (personalities, experience), the type of project (precedent-edness, difficulty, new or familiar domain, complexity), and its environment (budget, schedule, politics, criticality). From this information, the "right" weight of process may be created.

Risk is the key   Analyzing the project risks is an effective way to help managers and practitioners determine the right weight of process. Risk can include schedule slip, cost overrun, technical failure, or unacceptable reduced capability. The essence of using risk to balance agility and discipline is to apply one simple question to nearly every facet of process within a project:

> Is it riskier for me to apply (more of) this process component or to refrain from applying it?

Based on our experience with a variety of large and small software projects, we believe that asking this question and honestly evaluating the answer can lead to the definition of reasonable, practical, and effective hybrids that balance discipline and agility. This book is our best effort to convince you of this, and to provide you with a framework and set of techniques for realizing balance within your organization.

2

Contrasts and Home Grounds

The complex nature of software development and the wide variety of methods make comparison of agile and plan-driven approaches difficult and imprecise. Nevertheless, we have found several important software project characteristics for which there are clear differences between agile and plan-driven methods. These are

- *Application characteristics,* including primary project goals, project size, and application environment.
- *Management characteristics,* including customer relations, planning and control, and project communications.
- *Technical characteristics,* including approaches to requirements definition, development, and test.
- *Personnel characteristics,* including customer characteristics, developer characteristics, and organizational culture.

Comparison is difficult and imprecise

In this chapter we discuss how agile and plan-driven methods approach each of these characteristics, giving examples to illustrate the differences. From that discussion, we consolidate our observations into specific home grounds for agile and plan-driven methods, and identify five critical factors that can be used to determine how a project or organization relates to those home grounds.

For those interested, Appendix E provides a summary of the small but growing body of empirical data available on agile and new plan-driven methods.

Application Characteristics

We have found a number of differences in the type of projects where each of the approaches has been successful. One area of difference is the appropriateness of the goals of each approach to those of the project. Other areas include the size of the project in terms of people, complexity and volume of software, and the type of business environment within which the project is developed.

Primary Goals

Agile goals are rapid value and responsiveness

The primary goals of agile methods are *rapid value* and *responsiveness to change.* The first of the 12 Agile Manifesto principles states, "Our highest priority is to satisfy the customer through early and continuous delivery of valuable software." Agile projects generally do not perform return-on-investment analyses to determine an optimal allocation of resources to deliver specific value. They prefer to build things quickly and find out through experience what activity or feature will add the most value next. This laissez-faire approach generally avoids the loss of large investments pursued on faulty assumptions, but can lead to local or short-term optimization problems that may impact the project adversely later on.

The fourth Agile Manifesto value proposition prefers "responding to change over following a plan." This is a reactive posture rather than a proactive strategy. In a world characterized by rapid changes in the marketplace, technology, or environment, such a reactive posture has considerable advantages over being locked into an obsolete plan. One downside is that reactive management with a flighty customer can result in an unstable, chaotic project. Another potential downside is an overemphasis on tactical over strategic objectives.

Reactive posture has advantages where change is rapid, but some risk

The primary goals of plan-driven methods are *predictability, stability,* and *high assurance.* The plans, work products, and verification and validation strategies of plan-driven methods support these goals. Process improvement, as represented by the SW-CMM and CMMI, focuses on predictability and stability by increasing process capability through standardization, measurement, and control. Prediction is based on the measurements of prior standard activities. Control is asserted when the current progress is outside of expected tolerances.

Plan-driven goals are predictability, stability, and high assurance

For relatively stable projects, the proactive investments in process and up-front plans by organizations implementing the CMM or CMMI can achieve predictability, stability, and high assurance. However, when confronted with unprecedented projects and high rates of unforeseeable change, these organizations find that predictability and stability degrade, and the project incurs significant expenditures in keeping processes relevant and plans up to date.

Proactive posture is effective with stability

For high-assurance, safety-critical projects, following a thorough, documented set of plans and specifications is the only way to meet existing certification standards such as RTCA DO-178B. These standards require strict adherence to process and specific types of documentation to achieve safety or security.

Plans and specifications are required for certification

Size

Agile works best on smaller projects

Currently, agile processes seem to work best with *small to medium* teams of people working on relatively small applications. In his landmark XP book, Kent Beck says, "Size clearly matters. You probably couldn't run an XP project with a hundred programmers. Not fifty. Nor twenty, probably. Ten is definitely doable."[1] The general consensus is that the tight coordination and shared knowledge generally prevents agile methods with teams over forty.[2, 3]

Scaling up has proven difficult

⊞ See Appendix E3

There have been occasional successful larger agile projects with up to 250 people. The highly successful 50-person Singapore lending application, and another successful 250-person banking application,[4] are good examples. However, the manager of both confessed, "I would never do [a 250-person project] again. It was way too big." The largest project to date used Scrum to develop a corporate portfolio of related applications involving around 800 developers at IDX, a medical information services company.[5] As shown in the 50-person XP case study in Chapter 4, a larger agile project needs to adopt traditional plans and specifications in order to deal with the increasingly complex, multi-dimensional interactions among the project's elements.

Traditional rigor is more effective on large projects

Traditional plan-driven methods scale better to *large* projects. The plans, documentation, and processes provide for better communication and coordination across large groups. However, a bureaucratic, plan-driven organization that requires an average of one person-month just to get a project authorized and started is not going to be very efficient on small projects.

Plan-driven is a necessity on large complex projects

For the extremely large, path-breaking U.S. Army/DARPA Future Combat Systems program, our Software Steering Committee recently participated in a 150-person, week-long review of the completeness and consistency of thousands of pages of specifications. The specifications dealt with 34 highly complex system elements such as robotic combat vehicles and integrated command-control vehicles. They were produced by multiple integrated product teams and were about to be released for subcontractor bids. The process produced around 2,000 problem reports, many of which, if issued in their current state, would have caused person-years of rework. We see no way to avoid an activity of this nature on extremely large systems of systems, and absolutely no way to handle the problem with agile standup meetings and tacit knowledge propagation.

Environment

Agile approaches "are most applicable to *turbulent, high-change* environments," and have a world view that organizations are complex adaptive systems, in which requirements are emergent rather than pre-specifiable.[6] However, "welcome changing requirements, even late in development," can be misapplied with disastrous results. One of the authors was involved in a review of software-caused rocket vehicle failures. The main cause by far was the inadequate testing, verification, and configuration management of last-minute changes—i.e., responding to change over following a plan.

Agile approaches are comfortable in high-change environments— with some risks

Agile methods concentrate on delivering a specific software product, on time, that completely satisfies a customer. As such, the scope of concern is focused on the *product at hand* and generally ignores problems that may occur later. There is little, if any, concern with the organization beyond the project except as supporting or interfering with the development. This works well at the project level, but as some users have found, ". . . early experience with elements of XP on departmental applications produced code that didn't integrate well with [the] company's overall infrastructure or scale in production."[7]

Agile focuses on the product at hand

Agile successes have largely been in in-house environments

Agile methods have been almost entirely performed within in-house or dedicated development environments.[8] This makes it easier to have a close relationship to local users, but harder to perform various forms of distributed development, evolution, and usage.

Agile assumes flexible user system to accommodate evolution

Problems in applying an agile approach can manifest because it is assumed that the user's operational system will be flexible enough to accommodate unplanned evolution paths.[9,10] This assumption fails in several circumstances:

- The need to overcome stovepipes, where several independently evolved applications must subsequently be closely integrated.
- "Information-sclerosis" cases, where temporary procedural work-arounds caused by software deficiencies solidify into unchangeable constraints on system evolution and can cause unnecessary rework. The following comment is a typical example: "It's nice that you reprogrammed the software and changed those equipment codes to make them more intelligible for us, but the Codes Committee just met and established the current codes as company standards."
- Bridging situations, where the new software is incrementally replacing a large existing system. If the existing system is poorly modularized, it is difficult to undo the old software in ways that fit the expanding increments of new software.
- Monolithic requirements, such as the need for critical-mass core capabilities. For example, delivering 20 percent of an aircraft flight control module might not be practical.
- Continuity requirements, where you must maintain familiarity with the system across a large, mission-critical user base. Consider the safety risks in making significant monthly changes to air traffic controllers' operational procedures.

Plan-driven methods work best when the *requirements are largely determinable in advance* (including via prototyping) and remain *relatively stable.* Change rates on the order of 1 percent of the requirements per month are acceptable. Unfortunately, in the increasingly frequent situations where the rate of change is much higher than this, traditional methods designed for stable software begin to unravel. Time-consuming processes to ensure complete, consistent, precise, testable, and traceable requirements will face possibly insurmountable problems keeping up with the changes.

Plan-driven methods need stability

Plan-driven methods also cover a broader spectrum of activities than agile methods. Often used in contracted software development, they can address product line, organizational, and enterprise concerns that span multiple projects. In order to better handle this broader spectrum, plan-driven methods anticipate (plan for) future needs through architectures and extensible designs. They develop capabilities in related disciplines (e.g., systems engineering, human factors) and expect to impact a large number of people at various levels within the organizational hierarchy. Plan-driven organizations also usually exhibit a strong, quantitative process improvement focus.

Plan-driven scope includes system engineering, organization, outsourcing

See Appendix E3

Management Characteristics

There are a number of differences in the approaches with respect to how they are managed and to the expectations each has for the customer and other stakeholders. Planning, control, and communication are crucial to success, but are approached differently by the agile and plan-driven camps.

Customer Relations

Agile encourages a dedicated collocated customer

Agile methods strongly depend on *dedicated, collocated customer* representatives to keep the project focused on adding rapid value to the organization. This generally works very well at the project level.

The main agile stress point is the interface between the customer representative and the users

To succeed, agile customer representatives must be in synch with both the system users they represent and the development team. As will be seen in the lease management case study in Chapter 4, problems can arise when the representative does not accurately reflect the needs and desires of the users through lack of understanding or failure to keep abreast of the user concerns. Thus the customer representative becomes the primary stress point for agile methods.

Plan-driven methods depend on contracts and specifications

Plan-driven methods generally depend on some form of *contract* between the developers and customers as the basis for customer relations. They try to cope with foreseeable problems by working through them in advance and formalizing the solutions in a documented agreement. This has some advantages, particularly in stable situations. The developers know what they have to do. The customers know what they are getting and are better able to continue with their operational responsibilities. This maintains their operational knowledge and increases their value when they exercise prototypes or review progress and plans.

The main plan-driven stress point is the interface between the developer and the customer

However, the contract makes the developer-customer interface the major stress point for plan-driven methods. A precise contract causes startup delays and is harder to adapt to needed changes. An imprecise contract can create incompatible expectations, leading to adversarial relations and lack of trust. The worst case is when a tight, fixed-price contract results in the lawyers negotiating changes rather than the problem-solvers. Creative award-fee or profit-sharing contracts can help, but the presence of the contract remains a potential stress point on developer-customer trust.

For a project to succeed, the stakeholders must trust that the developing organization will perform the needed work for the available, agreed-to resources. Agile developers use *working software and customer participation* to instill trust in their track record, the systems they've developed, and the expertise of their people. This is one of the reasons agile projects have been primarily used for in-house development. It takes time to build up the level of trust required for the customer and developer to minimize contractual safeguards and detailed specifications. In many software development sectors, that length of time is simply not available.

Agile developers use working software to build customer trust

Plan-driven people count on their *process maturity* to provide confidence in their work. CMM appraisals are often used in source selection for large system implementation or for sourcing decisions, but one shouldn't assume documented plans guarantee the project will follow them. Although customers often feel secure when contracting with a SW-CMM Level 5 organization for software development, there have been a number of cases where the trust was misplaced. In several instances, particularly with offshore software organizations, customers have discovered that the "Level 5" software teams they hired were in fact raw, untrained new hires with little knowledge of CMM practices. Trust, in both plans and people, can have its limits.

Plan-driven developers use established process maturity to build customer trust

Planning and Control

In the agile world, planning is seen as a *means to an end* rather than a means of recording in text. Agilists estimate that their projects spend about 20 percent of their time planning or replanning. The agile projects' speed and agility come largely from deliberate group planning efforts that enable operation on the basis of tacit interpersonal knowledge rather than explicit documented knowledge as represented in plans and specifications. Many of the agile practices—pair programming, daily standup

Agilists see planning as a means to an end

all-hands meetings, shared code ownership, collocated developers and customers, team planning—are as much about developing the team's shared tacit knowledge base as they are about getting work done. When unforeseen changes come, the team members can call upon their shared vision of the project's goals and their shared understanding of the software content to quickly develop and implement a revised solution. As the project scales up, however, this becomes increasingly difficult.

Plan-driven methods use plans to communicate and coordinate

Plan-driven methods use plans to *anchor their processes* and *provide broad-spectrum communication*. Plans make up a large portion of the required documentation in most plan-driven approaches. Plan-driven methods rely heavily on documented process plans (schedules, milestones, procedures) and product plans (requirements, architecture, standards) to keep everyone coordinated. Individual plans are often produced for specific activities and then integrated into "master plans."

Both use past performance to inform planning

Considerable effort is spent on maintaining historical data so that planning projections can be more accurate. The fundamental measure of progress is tracking of progress against plans. Planning is done and adjusted constantly. Plans make explicit the expectations and relationships between various project efforts, and between the project and other independently evolving systems. Remember, however, that for rapidly evolving systems, the more detailed the plans, the more expensive and time consuming the rework.

Agile is "planning driven," rather than "plan-driven"

With respect to distinctions in how agile and traditional methods process plans, Kent Beck, cocreator of XP, agreed with the distinctions in the following e-mail to us:

> I think the phrase "plan driven" is the key. I would characterize XP as "planning driven" in contrast. What XP teams find valuable is the collaboration, elicitation,

and balancing of priorities in the planning act itself. The plans that result have a short half-life, not because they are bad plans, but because their underlying . assumptions have a short half-life.

Project Communication

Agile methods rely heavily on *tacit, interpersonal knowledge* for their success. They cultivate the development and use of tacit knowledge, depending on the understanding and experience of the people doing the work and their willingness to share it. Knowledge is specifically gathered through team planning and project reviews (an activity agilists refer to as "retrospection"). It is shared across the organization as experienced people work on more tasks with different people.

Agile methods depend on tacit knowledge

Agile methods generally rely on more frequent, person-to-person communication. As stated in the Agile Manifesto, emphasis is given to "individuals and interactions." Few of the agile communication channels are one-way, showing a preference for collaboration. Standup meetings, pair programming, and the planning game are all examples of the agile communication style and its investments in developing shared tacit knowledge.

Communication is person-to-person and frequent

Relying completely on tacit knowledge is like performing without a safety net. While things go well, you avoid the extra baggage and setup effort, but there may be situations that will make you wish for that net. Assuming that everyone's tacit knowledge is consistent across a large team is risky, and as people start rotating off the team, the risk gets higher.

Relying on tacit knowledge can be risky

At some point, a group's ability to function exclusively on tacit knowledge will run up against well-known scalability laws for group communication. For a team with N members, there are $N(N-1)/2$ different interpersonal communication paths to keep up to date. Even broadcast

Tacit knowledge is difficult to scale

techniques, such as standup group meetings and hierarchical team-of-teams techniques, run into serious scalability problems. Consider the previously discussed Future Combat Systems subcontractor specification reviews as an example of a limiting case.

Plan-driven approaches use explicit, documented knowledge

Plan-driven methods rely heavily on *explicit documented knowledge*. With plan-driven methods, communication tends to be one-way. Communication is generally from one entity to another rather than between two entities. Process descriptions, progress reports, and the like are nearly always communicated as unidirectional flow.

Agile and plan-driven methods use both kinds of knowledge

We should note that this distinction between "agile-tacit" and "plan-driven-explicit" is not absolute. Agile methods' source code and test cases certainly qualify as explicit documented knowledge, and even the most rigorous plan-driven method does not try to get along without some interpersonal communication to ensure consistent, shared understanding of documentation intent and semantics.

Agile adds documentation when needed while plan-driven methods generally subtract what is not needed

When agile methods employ documentation, they emphasize doing the minimum essential amount. Unfortunately, most plan-driven methods suffer from a "tailoring-down" syndrome, which is sadly reinforced by most government procurement regulations. These plan-driven methods are developed by experts, who want them to provide users with guidance for most or all foreseeable situations. The experts therefore make them very comprehensive, but "tailorable-down" for less critical or less complex situations. The experts understand tailoring the methods and often provide guidelines and examples for others to use.

Once specified, removing documentation is difficult

Unfortunately, less expert and less self-confident developers, customers, and managers tend to see the full-up set of plans, specifications, and standards as a security blanket. At this point a sort of Gresham's Law

("Bad money drives out good money") takes over, and the least-expert participant generally drives the project to use the full-up set of documents rather than an appropriate subset. While the nonexperts rarely read the ever-growing stack of documents, they will maintain a false sense of security in the knowledge they have followed best practice to ensure project predictability and control. Needless to say, the expert methodologists are then frustrated with how their tailorable methods are used—and usually verbally abused—by developers and acquirers alike.

This process has been going on for decades, in the United States from MIL-STD-1679 through -2167, -2167A, and -498, and through IEEE/EIA-016 and 12207. It is currently seen in nongovernment methods such as RUP, TSP, and one of the authors' methods, MBASE. Both authors thank the agilists for making it clear that a better approach to plan-driven methods is needed.

Shortfalls of tailor-down methods have been known for decades

Technical Characteristics

Technical characteristics have been the focus of much of the debate as to the effectiveness of agile and plan-driven methods. This section looks at how each of the approaches handles requirements elicitation and management, development activities, and testing.

Requirements

Most agile methods express requirements in terms of *adjustable, informal stories*. Agile methods count on their rapid iteration cycles to determine needed changes in the desired capability and to fix them in the next iteration. Determining the highest-priority set of requirements to be included in the next iteration is done collaboratively by the customers and developers. The customers express their strongest needs and the developers assess what combinations of capabilities are feasible for

Agile uses informal, user-prioritized stories as requirements

inclusion in the next development iteration (typically on the order of a month). Negotiations establish the contents of the next iteration.

Plan-driven methods prefer specific, formalized requirements

Plan-driven methods generally prefer *formally baselined, complete, consistent, traceable, and testable specifications.* For some time, the plan-driven world has been aware of collaborative requirements determination[11] but has been slow to respond. Because it was developed when the accepted practice was for the systems engineers to identify, define, and hand off the software requirements, the SW-CMM states, "Analysis and allocation of the system requirements is not the responsibility of the software engineering group but is a prerequisite for their work."[12]

Prioritization has not been widely used in plan-driven approaches

The plan-driven world has also been much slower than the agile world to assimilate new concepts such as prioritized requirements and evolutionary requirements. Some progress is being made with the introduction of the CMMI product suite because it extends beyond that of the SW-CMM. CMMI includes integrated teaming, requirements development, and risk management, all of which support the use of risk-driven, evolving requirements specifications over the traditional "complete" requirements specifications and their limitations.

Risk-driven approaches are similar to agile

Risk-driven approaches assert it is better not to specify elements where the risks of specifying them are larger than the risks of *not* specifying them.[13] For example, prematurely specifying a detailed graphical user interface runs the risk of breakage due to changing requirements, systems that are not responsive to the users, and solutions that can't evolve as the understanding of the system and its operational concept matures. The only risk in *not* specifying it is that it may take a few more passes with an automated interface creation tool. So, risk-driven approaches would rather you not specify the user interface early on.

The opposite case might apply to a mission-critical function or security requirement.

On the other hand, the plan-driven world is considerably ahead of the agile world in dealing with quality or nonfunctional requirements such as reliability, throughput, real-time deadline satisfaction, or scalability. These become increasingly important for large, mission-critical systems and are a source of expensive architecture breakers when an initial simple design doesn't scale up. Most agilists participating in a recent Center for Empirically Based Software Engineering (CeBASE)* eWorkshop on this topic tended to consider a quality attribute as just another feature to be easily dealt with. Most plan-driven developers consider quality attributes as a range of system-level properties affecting many features and extremely difficult to "add on." We'll discuss this more in the next section.

Plan-driven methods handle nonfunctional requirements better

Development

The primary difference between agile and plan-driven development practices deal with the design and architecture of the software. Agile methods advocate *simple design,* one that emerges as functionality is implemented. Simple design can be characterized by XP's goal to "always have the simplest design that runs the current test suite."[14] Agilists encourage the developer to make the design simpler at every opportunity. Taken to its logical conclusion, this means if your design has capabilities that are beyond the current user stories or that anticipate new features, you should expend extra effort to remove them. Of course, the idea is not to have them there in the first place.

Agile advocates simple design

*CeBASE is an NSF-sponsored collaborative research institute led by the University of Maryland's Fraunhofer Center for Experimental Software Engineering and the University of Southern California's Center for Software Engineering. Its mission is to strengthen and propagate the results of empirical research in software engineering (http://www.cebase.org/).

Simple design depends on low-cost rework and rapid change

The basis for advocating simple design rests on two fundamental assertions. The first is that the cost of rework to change the software ("refactoring" in agile language) to support new, possibly unanticipated, capabilities will remain low over time. The second fundamental assumption is that the application situation will change so rapidly that any code added to support future capabilities will never be used.

Low-cost rework is not guaranteed with agile methods

⊠ See Appendix E1

The assertion concerning low-cost rework is based on the hypothesis that constant refactoring yields constant improvement, so there will be a constant, low rate of change rather than a few large, expensive redesigns. Unfortunately, this seems to be a fragile proposition. Experiences where the cost to change has remained low over time tend to be anecdotal, associated with smaller applications, and usually involve expert programmers who are able to quickly refactor the design and correct defects. But the only sources of empirical data we have encountered have come from less-expert early adopters who found that even for small applications, the percentage of effort spent on refactoring and correcting defects increases with the number of requirement stories.[15, 16]

Low-cost rework doesn't scale

Experience to date also indicates that low-cost refactoring cannot be depended upon as projects scale up. The most serious problems that arise with simple design are problems known as "architecture breakers." These highly expensive problems can occur when early, simple design decisions result in foreseeable changes that cause breakage in the design beyond the ability of refactoring to handle. Here are some examples of architecture breakers.

■ An early commitment to a fourth-generation language and its infrastructure that works beautifully when the application and user base are small, but is impossible to scale up as the application and user base become large.

■ Escalating reliability, throughput, response time, or other quality attributes during development, or the addition of functionality within a tightly specified, real-time control loop that cannot be accommodated within the design. Frequently, the best performing architecture has only a limited range with respect to the level of quality specified.[17, 18]

■ Deferred implementation of special conditions or functions, such as multinational and multilingual operations, fault tolerance through processor failover, or the need to handle extra-long messages, that significantly impact many parts of the software.

The second assumption concerning rapid change addresses programming efficiency. The thought here is that adding hooks for future functionality unnecessarily complicates the design and increases the effort to develop subsequent increments. Within the XP and other agile communities, this concept is known as You Aren't Going to Need It (YAGNI). YAGNI works fine when future requirements are largely unpredictable, but can be highly inefficient where there is a reasonable understanding of future needs. In situations where future requirements are predictable, YAGNI both throws away valuable architectural support for foreseeable requirements and frustrates customers who want developers to believe their priorities and evolution requirements are worth accommodating.

Simple design implies YAGNI— You Aren't Going to Need It

Plan-driven methods use *planning* and *architecture-based design* to accommodate foreseeable change. This effort allows the designers to organize the system to take advantage of software reuse across product lines and can have a major impact on rapid development.

Plan-driven methods advocate architecture to anticipate changes

In one division, Hewlett-Packard was able to reduce its software development cycle time from 48 months to 12 months over 5 years, by developing plug-and-play reusable software modules.[19] Significantly,

HP had excellent results with product line architecture

Hewlett-Packard also found that its reuse economic model needed to add costs for adapting product line assets to unforeseeable change.[20] These included cost factors for architectural update, component obsolescence, and adaptive maintenance of components to stay consistent with changing external interfaces. Even with these added costs, software product lines have been highly successful for HP and many other organizations.[21, 22, 23]

Architecture can waste resources in rapidly changing environments

See Appendix E2

Thus, for the levels of predictability and dependability that are primary objectives of plan-driven methods, a significant amount of effort goes into analyzing and defining a robust architecture that will accommodate the system's envisioned life cycle usage envelope. For small and rapidly changing applications, this level of architecture investment, sometimes referred to as Big Design Up Front (BDUF), will be overkill. Several agile methods use some level of architecting: Crystal, DSDM, FDD, and Lean Development, for example. Scrum's consideration of its requirement backlog helps avoid misinformed simple design.

Other agile practices can support plan-driven approaches

While simple design and architectural design are definitely conflicting approaches, there are some agile development practices that can readily and productively be adopted for plan-driven projects. Examples are evolutionary and incremental development, continuous integration, and pair programming.

Testing

Agile methods develop tests before code, and test incrementally

Testing is one way of validating that the customers have specified the right product and verifying that the developers have built the product right. It requires that the code be developed and executed, which means that for long developments, problems will not be discovered until late in the development cycle, when they are expensive to fix. Agile methods address this problem by organizing the development into short increments, and by applying pair programming or other review techniques to remove more code defects as they are being generated. They also develop executable tests to serve in place of requirements and to enable earlier and continuous regression testing. Automated testing support is recommended by most agile methods. This approach has a number of significant advantages.

See Appendix E1

- It ensures that the requirements are testable.
- It avoids a great deal of documentation for requirements, requirement/test matrices, and test case definitions.
- It enables incremental build-and-test, with earlier identification of defects and misinterpreted stories.
- It helps modularize the applications structure and provides a safety net for refactoring.
- It helps form an explicit working knowledge of the application.[24]

However, there are some risks inherent to the test-first approach.[25]

- Rapid change causes expensive breakage in the tests.
- Rapid change causes mismatches and race problems between the code and the tests.
- Lack of applications or testing expertise may produce inadequate test coverage.

Plan-driven methods address the expensive late-fix problem by developing and consistency-checking requirements and architecture specifications early in the development process. They also invest in automated test suites to support the considerable planning and preparation before running tests. This creates a good deal of documentation that may undergo breakage due to changing requirements, but the documentation rework effort will usually be less than the test rework effort, particularly with automated test suites. On the other hand, late testing misses much

Plan-driven methods test to specifications

of the agile early-testing advantages cited above. Plan-driven methods also frequently manifest an independent (and often adversarial) testing bureaucracy that can be entirely divorced from developer and customer, and so may spend a good proportion of scarce project resources determining if the product matches the letter of the specifications rather than operational intent and customer need.

Personnel Characteristics

While there has been significant discussion of the technical differences between agile and plan-driven approaches, we believe that some of the most fundamental differences lie in the people issues. The customers, developers, and organizational cultures have a significant influence on the success of most projects. In this section we discuss how the approaches are reliant on specific characteristics in each of these areas.

Customers

There is significant risk in unsuitable customer representatives

In the "Customer Relations" section above, we concluded that the major difference between agile and plan-driven methods was that agile methods strongly emphasize having dedicated and collocated customer representatives, while plan-driven methods count on a good deal of up-front, customer-developer work on contractual plans and specifications. For agile methods, the greatest risk is that insistence on a dedicated, collocated customer representative will cause the customer organization to supply the person that is most expendable. This risk establishes the need for criteria to determine the adequacy of customer representatives.

In our critical success factor analysis of over 100 e-services projects at USC, we have found that success depends on having customer representatives who are Collaborative, Representative, Authorized, Committed, and Knowledgeable (CRACK) performers. If the customer representatives are not collaborative, they will sow discord and frustration, resulting in the loss of team morale. If they are not representative, they will lead the developers to deliver unacceptable products. If they are not authorized, they will incur delays seeking authorization or, even worse, lead the project astray by making unauthorized commitments. If they are not committed, they won't do the necessary homework and won't be there when the developers need them most. Finally, if they are not knowledgeable, they will cause delays, unacceptable products, or both.

USC found customer representatives need to be Collaborative, Representative, Authorized, Committed, and Knowledgeable (CRACK)

This summary of customer impact on the landmark C3 project, considered to be the first XP project, is a good example of the need for CRACK customer representatives.

Chrysler provides an example

> The on-site customer in this project had a vision of the perfect system she wanted to develop. She was able to provide user stories that were easy to estimate. Moreover, she was with the development team every day, answering any business questions the developer had.
>
> Half-way [through] the project, several things changed, which eventually led to the project being cancelled. One of the changes was the replacement of the on-site customer, showing that the actual way in which the customer is involved is one of the key success factors in an XP project. The new on-site customer was present most of the time, just like the previous on-site customer, and available to the development team for questions. Unfortunately, the requirements and user stories were not as crisp as they were before.[26]

Plan-driven methods also need CRACK customer representatives and benefit from full-time, on-site participation. Good planning artifacts, however, enable them to settle for part-time CRACK representatives who provide further benefits by keeping active in customer operations. The greatest customer challenge for plan-driven methods is to keep project control from falling into the hands of overly bureaucratic

Plan-driven methods also need CRACK customers, but not full-time

contract managers who prioritize contract compliance above getting project results.

FAA example of bureaucratic plan-driven approach

A classic example of customer bureaucracy is provided in Robert Britcher's book, *The Limits of Software,*[27] describing his experience on perhaps the world's biggest failed software project: the FAA/IBM Advanced Automation System for U.S. national air traffic control. Due to many bureaucratic and other problems, including responding to change over following a plan, the project was overrunning by years and billions of dollars. One of the software development groups came up with a way of reducing the project's commitment to a heavyweight brand of software inspections that were slowing the project down by consuming too much staff effort in paperwork and redundant tasks. The group came up with a lightweight version of the inspection process. It was comparably successful in finding defects, but with much less time and effort. Was the group rewarded for doing this? No, the contracting bureaucracy sent them a cease-and-desist letter faulting them for contract noncompliance and ordering them to go back to the heavyweight inspections. This is the kind of plan-driven bureaucracy that agilists justifiably deride.

Developers

Agile developers need more than technical skills

Critical people-factors for agile methods include amicability, talent, skill, and communication.[28] An independent assessment identifies this as a potential problem for agile methods: "There are only so many Kent Becks in the world to lead the team. All of the agile methods put a premium on having premium people . . ."[29] Figure 2-1 distinguishes the most effective operating points of agile and plan-driven projects.[30, 31] Both operate best with a mix of developer skills and understanding, but agile methods tend to need a richer mix of higher-skilled people.

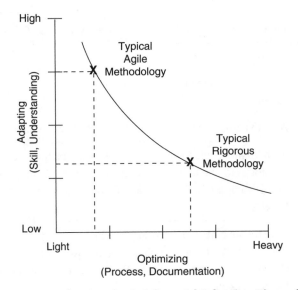

**Figure 2-1   Balancing Optimizing and Adapting Dimensions
(from Cockburn and Highsmith)**

When you have such people available on your project, statements like "A few designers sitting together can produce a better design than each could produce alone" are valid. If not, you're more likely to get design-by-committee, with the opposite effect. The plan-driven methods of course do better with great people, but are generally more able to plan the project and architect the software so that less-capable people can contribute with low risk. A significant consideration here is the unavoidable statistic that 49.999 percent of the world's software developers are below average (slightly more precisely, below median).

Plan-driven methods need fewer highly talented people than agile

It is important to be able to classify the type of personnel required for success in the various methods. Alistair Cockburn has addressed levels of skill and understanding required for performing various method-related functions, such as using, tailoring, adapting, or revising a method.

We modify Cockburn's levels to meet our needs

Table 2-1 Levels of Software Method Understanding and Use (after Cockburn)	
Level	**Characteristics**
3	Able to revise a method (break its rules) to fit an unprecedented new situation
2	Able to tailor a method to fit a precedented new situation
1A	With training, able to perform discretionary method steps (e.g., sizing stories to fit increments, composing patterns, compound refactoring, complex COTS integration). With experience, can become Level 2.
1B	With training, able to perform procedural method steps (e.g., coding a simple method, simple refactoring, following coding standards and CM procedures, running tests). With experience, can master some Level 1A skills.
−1	May have technical skills, but unable or unwilling to collaborate or follow shared methods.

Drawing on the three levels of understanding in Aikido (Shu-Ha-Ri), he has identified three levels of software method understanding that help sort out what various levels of people can be expected to do within a given method framework.[32] Modifying his work to meet our needs, we have split his Level 1 to address some distinctions between agile and plan-driven methods, and added an additional level to address the problem of method-disrupters. Our version is provided in Table 2-1.

Reassign Level -1s   Level −1 people should be rapidly identified and reassigned to work other than performing on either agile or plan-driven teams.

Level 1B people are average-and-below, less-experienced, hard-working developers. They can function well in performing straightforward software development in a stable situation. But they are likely to slow down an agile team trying to cope with rapid change, particularly if they form a majority of the team. They can form a well-performing majority of a stable, well-structured plan-driven team.

Level 1Bs need considerable guidance, work well in plan-driven environment

Level 1A people can function well on agile or plan-driven teams if there are enough Level 2 people to guide them. When agilists refer to being able to succeed on agile teams with ratios of five Level 1 people per Level 2 person, they are generally referring to Level 1A people.

Level 1As need guidance but can work well on agile teams

Level 2 people can function well in managing a small, precedented agile or plan-driven project but need the guidance of Level 3 people on a large or unprecedented project. Some Level 2s have the capability to become Level 3s with experience. Some do not.

Level 2s can manage precedented projects but need Level 3 guidance on unprecedented projects

Culture

In an agile culture, the people feel comfortable and empowered when there are *many degrees of freedom* available for them to define and work problems. This is the classic craftsman environment, where each person is expected and trusted to do whatever work is necessary to the success of the project. This includes looking for common or unnoticed tasks and completing them.

Agilists like many degrees of freedom

In a plan-driven culture, the people feel comfortable and empowered when there are *clear policies and procedures* that define their role in the enterprise. This is more of a production-line environment where each person's tasks are well-defined. The expectation is that they will accomplish the tasks to specification so that their work products will easily

Plan-driven people need clear process and roles

integrate into others' work products with limited knowledge of what others are actually doing.

Cultural inertia is a significant challenge

These cultures get reinforced as people tend to self-select for their preferred culture, and as people within the culture get promoted to higher levels of management. Once a culture is well established, it is difficult and time consuming to change. This cultural inertia may be the most significant challenge to the integration of agile and plan-driven approaches.

Agile culture change has a revolutionary flavor

To date, agile culture change has had a bottom-up, revolutionary flavor. Failing projects with no hope of success have been the usual pilots, supported by an "it can't hurt" attitude from management and a "no challenge is too hard" adrenalin-charged response from practitioners. Successes have been extraordinary in many cases and have been used to defend migration to less troubled projects.

CMM faced culture change issues early

Early CMM adopters faced similar challenges, although there was early involvement of middle management. The concept of culture change evolved rapidly and is now well understood by the managers and Software Engineering Process Groups (SEPGs). These have been the main change agents in evolving their organizations from following improvised, ad hoc processes toward following plan-driven, CMM-compliant processes.

CMMI improves CMM, but is a culture change in itself

The new CMMI upgrades the SW-CMM in more agile directions, with new process areas for integrated teaming, risk management, and overall integrated systems and software engineering. A number of organizations are welcoming this opportunity to add more agility to their organizational culture. But others that retain a more bureaucratic interpretation of the SW-CMM are facing the challenge of "change-averse change agents" who have become quite comfortable in their bureaucratic culture.

Summary

This chapter has provided a lot of information on a number of characteristics. In the following section we summarize the material and provide a graphic way to use the characteristics to describe the agility/plan-driven profile of a project or organization in terms of five factors.

Home Grounds

Table 2-2 summarizes the comparisons in the four areas of Chapter 2 by showing the "home grounds" for agile and plan-driven methods—the sets of conditions under which they are most likely to succeed. The more a particular project's conditions differ from the home ground conditions,

Home grounds can also characterize projects

Table 2-2 Agile and Plan-Driven Method Home Grounds		
Characteristics	**Agile**	**Plan-Driven**
Application		
Primary Goals	Rapid value; responding to change	Predictability, stability, high assurance
Size	Smaller teams and projects	Larger teams and projects
Environment	Turbulent; high change; project-focused	Stable; low-change; project/organization focused
Management		
Customer Relations	Dedicated on-site customers; focused on prioritized increments	As-needed customer interactions; focused on contract provisions
Planning and Control	Internalized plans; qualitative control	Documented plans, quantitative control
Communication	Tacit interpersonal knowledge	Explicit documented knowledge
		(continued)

Table 2-2 Continued		
Characteristics	**Agile**	**Plan-Driven**
Technical		
Requirements	Prioritized informal stories and test cases; undergoing unforeseeable change	Formalized project, capability, interface, quality, foreseeable evolution requirements
Development	Simple design; short increments; refactoring assumed inexpensive	Extensive design; longer increments; refactoring assumed expensive
Testing	Executable test cases define requirements	Documented test plans and procedures
Personnel		
Customers	Dedicated, collocated CRACK* performers	CRACK* performers, not always collocated
Developers	At least 30% full-time Cockburn Level 2 and 3 experts; no Level 1B or -1 personnel**	50% Cockburn Level 3s early; 10% throughout; 30% Level 1Bs workable; no Level -1s**
Culture	Comfort and empowerment via many degrees of freedom (thriving on chaos)	Comfort and empowerment via framework of policies and procedures (thriving on order)

* Collaborative, Representative, Authorized, Committed, Knowledgeable
** These numbers will particularly vary with the complexity of the application

the more risk there is in using one approach in its pure form and the more valuable it is to blend in some of the complementary practices from the opposite method. In Chapter 4 we will provide case studies showing how an agile and a plan-driven project were able to succeed outside their home grounds. Chapter 5 illustrates a risk-driven approach for tailoring balanced agile/plan-driven strategies for non–home ground projects.

Misconceptions

Table 2-3 is an attempt to counter several misconceptions about agile and plan-driven methods. Many of these are caused by people misrepresenting their use of agile and plan-driven methods. A good example was presented in Chapter 1 where a team claimed to follow XP, but on further investigation had simply stopped documenting their software.[33]

People misrepresent both approaches

Such misconceptions propel agile and plan-driven advocates into a lot of unnecessary, polarized arguments and add to the perplexity that we are trying to help our readers sort out.

Misconceptions hurt everyone

Table 2-3 Misconceptions and Realities about Agile and Plan-Driven Methods	
Misconceptions	**Realities**
Plan-Driven Methods	
Plan-driven methods are uniformly bureaucratic	Overly bureaucratic cultures and methods can stultify software development
Having documented plans guarantees compliance with plans	Not necessarily
Plan-driven methods can succeed with a lack of talented people	Plan-driven methods can succeed with a smaller percentage of talented people
High maturity guarantees success	Explicit, documented plans provide more of a safety net than tacit plans
There are no penalties in applying plan-driven methods when change is unforeseeable	Plan-driven methods work best in accommodating foreseeable change
	(continued)

Table 2-3 Continued	
Misconceptions	**Realities**
Agile Methods	
Agile methods don't plan	Agile methods get much of their speed and agility through creating and exploiting tacit knowledge
Agile methods require uniformly talented people	Agile methods work best when there is a critical mass of highly talented people involved
Agile methods can make the slope of the cost-to-change vs. time curve uniformly flat	Agile methods can reduce the slope of the cost-to-change vs. time curve
YAGNI is a universally safe assumption, and won't alienate your customers	YAGNI helps handle unforeseeable change, but is risky when change is foreseeable

Five Critical Factors

Decision factors are size, criticality, dynamism, personnel, and culture

As a "summary of summaries," we have concluded that there are five critical factors involved in determining the relative suitability of agile or plan-driven methods in a particular project situation. These factors, described in Table 2-4, are the project's size, criticality, dynamism, personnel, and culture factors. As we shall see in Chapters 4 and 5, a project which is a good fit to agile or plan-driven for four of the factors, but not the fifth, is a project in need of risk assessment and likely some mix of agile and plan-driven methods.

Size, criticality, and culture map easily to home grounds

The five critical factors associated with the agile and plan-driven home grounds from Table 2-4 are summarized graphically in Figure 2-2. Of the five axes in the polar graph, *Size* and *Criticality* are similar to the

Table 2-4 The Five Critical Agility/Plan-Driven Factors

Factor	Agility Discriminators	Plan-Driven Discriminators
Size	Well-matched to small products and teams. Reliance on tacit knowledge limits scalability.	Methods evolved to handle large products and teams. Hard to tailor down to small projects.
Criticality	Untested on safety-critical products. Potential difficulties with simple design and lack of documentation.	Methods evolved to handle highly critical products. Hard to tailor down to low-criticality products.
Dynamism	Simple design and continuous refactoring are excellent for highly dynamic environments, but a source of potentially expensive rework for highly stable environments.	Detailed plans and Big Design Up Front excellent for highly stable environment, but a source of expensive rework for highly dynamic environments.
Personnel	Requires continuous presence of a critical mass of scarce Cockburn Level 2 or 3 experts. Risky to use non-agile Level 1B people.	Needs a critical mass of scarce Cockburn Level 2 and 3 experts during project definition, but can work with fewer later in the project —unless the environment is highly dynamic. Can usually accommodate some Level 1B people.
Culture	Thrives in a culture where people feel comfortable and empowered by having many degrees of freedom. (Thriving on chaos)	Thrives in a culture where people feel comfortable and empowered by having their roles defined by clear policies and procedures. (Thriving on order)

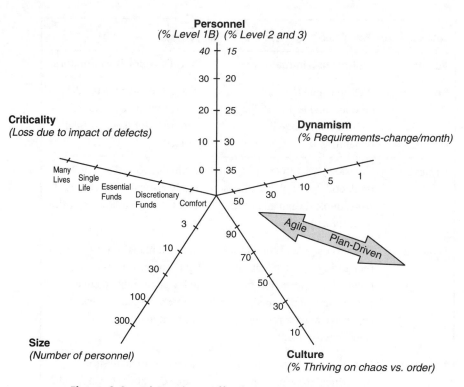

Figure 2-2   Dimensions Affecting Method Selection

factors used by Alistair Cockburn to distinguish between the lighter-weight Crystal methods (toward the center of the graph) and heavier-weight Crystal methods (toward the periphery). The *Culture* axis reflects the reality that agile methods will succeed better in a culture that "thrives on chaos"[34] than one that "thrives on order," and vice versa.

Dynamism reflects the rate of change, primarily a plan-driven issue

The other two axes are asymmetrical in that both agile and plan-driven methods are likely to succeed at one end, and only one of them is likely to succeed at the other. For *Dynamism,* agile methods are at home with both high and low rates of change, but plan-driven methods prefer low rates of change.

The *Personnel* scale refers to the extended Cockburn method skill rating scale discussed earlier in the chapter. Here the asymmetry is that while plan-driven methods can work well with both high and low skill levels, agile methods require a richer mix of higher-level skills (see Figure 2-1).

Personnel addresses mix of Level 2 and 3 and Level 1B developers

For example, a plan-driven project with 15 percent Level 2 and 3 people and 40 percent Level 1B people would initially use more than 15 percent Level 2 and 3 people to plan the project, but reduce the number thereafter. An agile project would have everybody working full-time, and the 15 percent Level 2s and 3s would be swamped trying to mentor the 40 percent Level 1Bs and the remaining Level 1As while trying to get their own work done as well.

A typical example of personnel mix

By rating a project along each of the five axes, you can visibly evaluate its home ground relationships. If all the ratings are near the center, you are in agile method territory. If they are at the periphery, you will best succeed with a plan-driven approach. If you are mostly in one or the other, you need to treat the exceptions as sources of risk and devise risk management approaches to address them.

Rating shows home ground relationship graphically

3

A Day in the Life

Agile and disciplined methods each have a vision of how software development *should* be.

So what does it feel like to develop software according to plan-driven or agile methods? In this chapter we try to portray the activities in a typical day on a software development project as performed by a plan-driven, PSP/TSP-trained team and by an agile, XP-trained team. First, we describe the activities of a typical day—one that falls well within the normal range of expected activities. Then we show how different the days might be if a significant event disrupts the normal activities—a crisis day. Finally, we discuss the similarities, differences, and implications of our two examples.

A typical day for plan-driven and agile methods

Typical Days

The typical day is based on a generic software development project. The product is a tool that processes a complex sales reporting and inventory management file. The file contains a large amount of data and

Both developing the same system

is automatically generated by a legacy system and delivered electronically to all relevant organizations. Data applicable to any one specific department is spread throughout the file, making it difficult for the department to manually extract the information it needs. The product under development will automatically break out the information needed by a specific department. A prototype has been developed, and the current project is to enhance the prototype and port it to another platform and operating system. The total project was initially estimated by the customer at around 20 thousand source lines of code (KSLOC) and approximately eight months' duration.

Friday of a typical week

While the activities are fictionalized, they are representative of the types of tasks undertaken on a typical project work day. We've selected Friday as an example day because it allows us to recap the week's work, thus showing a broader view of activities performed.

Background is provided

For each of the approaches, we identify the specific training that the participants have undergone in order to apply the method. We describe the preproject planning work that was undertaken and summarize the development environment and current status of the project. The team is identified, and we define any specific roles.

A Typical Day Using PSP/TSP*
Training

Considerable training is required

Each of the nine team members completed a 125-hour *PSP for Engineers* course, which provides the basic process, discipline, measurement, estimating, and quality management skills. Jan, the team leader, has participated in two TSP teams, one as Design Manager. She and

---

*Thanks to David Webb and his team from the Air Force Software Engineering Division of Hill Air Force Base and Dr. Tom Hilburn from Embry-Riddle Aeronautical University for support in the development of this section.

Fahad have completed the five-day TSP Launch Coach Training. Fahad, Greg, and Jim have also worked on TSP-based projects. Two of the members are familiar with the legacy system and two others have studied parts of the legacy documentation. Their assigned roles are shown in Table 3-1. Jan and Greg have Cockburn Level 2 skills. The other team members include five Level 1As and two Level 1Bs.

Table 3-1 PSP/TSP Roles		
Person	**Role**	**Responsibilities**
Jan	Team Leader	Leading team, ensuring engineers report process data, ensuring work is completed as planned.
Fran (and all team members)	Programmer/ Analyst	Developing requirements, design specifications, and software; reviewing designs and software; testing software; participating in inspections.
Fahad	Implementation Manager	Ensuring the implementation package is complete and ready for delivery.
Greg	Planning Manager	Supporting and guiding team members in planning and tracking their work.
Jim	Design Manager	Technical lead for developing and validating the overall architecture as well as package design.
Panitee	Quality/Process Manager	Defining process needs, making the quality plan, and tracking process and product quality.
Bashar	Support Manager	Determining, obtaining, and managing the tools needed to meet the team's technology and administrative support needs.
Margaret	Customer Interface Manager	Communicating with the customer.
Felipe	Test Manager	Package-level and integration testing.

Tools and Environment

Web-based data collection and standard OO tools

The team is using a Web-based tool to support PSP/TSP data collection and earned value reporting. The development environment is typical of object-oriented (OO) programming. Office layout is standard modular offices with each developer having a dedicated machine. A conference room with computer network and projection capabilities is available for meetings and inspections. There is a dedicated integration and test machine in an unoccupied cubicle.

Project Planning

Plans anchor TSP, but are routinely adjusted

At the beginning of the project, a four-day planning session (referred to as a TSP Launch workshop) was held with all the team members and the project management personnel. During the workshop the team defined the project goals, established team roles based on TSP role scripts (Figure 3-1 is an example of a role script from TSPi, Humphrey's instructional version of TSPi), defined the project processes, developed quality and support plans, and agreed on an overall product plan and schedule. Over 180 tasks were identified, estimated, and planned. Upper management, marketing, and customer representatives communicated their requirements to the team on the first day of the launch and agreed to the plan the team created on the final day of the launch.

Agile early, team is applying more rigor in development

The team recognized the need for considerable agility during the early prototyping phase of the project, and relaxed the requirements for specification change control, inspections, defect tracking, and statistical process control during that phase. This phase, however, is more critical to the delivery of the system, and so more of the TSP discipline is being applied.

Status

Nearing end of first phase

The project is in the third month, and a relaunch workshop is planned within the next two weeks. Nothing has been delivered, but a prototype

Objective	The Quality/Process Manager supports the team in defining the process needs, in making the quality plan, and in tracking process and product quality.
Role Characteristics	The characteristics most helpful to quality/process managers are the following. 1. You are concerned about software quality. 2. You are interested in process and process measurements. 3. You have some experience with or awareness of inspection and review methods. 4. You are willing and able to constructively review and comment on other people's work without antagonizing them.
Goals and Measures	Team member goal: Be a cooperative and effective team member. • Measures: Team PEER ratings for team spirit, overall contribution, and helpfulness and support Goal 1: All team members accurately report and properly use TSPi data. • Measure 1: The extent to which the team faithfully gathered and used all the required TSPi data Goal 2: The team faithfully follows the TSPi and produces a quality product. • Measure 2.1: How well the team followed the TSPi • Measure 2.2: How well the team's quality performance conformed to the quality plan • Measure 2.3: The degree to which you kept the team leader and instructor informed of quality problems • Measure 2.4: The degree to which you accomplished this goal without antagonizing the team or any team members Goal 3: All team inspections are properly moderated and reported. • Measure 3.1: All inspections were conducted according to the INS script and the team's quality standards. • Measure 3.2: INS forms are completed for all team inspections and all major defects reported on the owners' LOGD forms. Goal 4: All team meetings are accurately reported and the reports put in the project notebook. • Measure 4: The percentage of the team meetings with reports filed in the project notebook
Principal Activities	1. Lead the team in producing and tracking the quality plan. 2. Alert the team, the team leader, and the instructor to quality problems. 3. Lead the team in defining and documenting its processes and in maintaining the process improvement process. 4. Establish and maintain the team's development standards. 5. Review and approve all products before submission to the CCB. 6. Act as the team's inspection moderator. 7. Act as recorder in all the team's meetings. 8. Participate in producing the development cycle report. 9. Act as a development engineer.

Figure 3-1   TSPi Script for the Quality/Process Manager Role[1]

of the enhanced functionality has been demonstrated to management. Integration testing for the first phase is scheduled to begin next week.

The Day's Activities

8:30   Usually the team begins work on their planned tasks upon arrival. However, today, because of some organizational information that needs to be discussed, Jan gathers the group and provides a brief summary of her organizational staff meeting. While they are gathered, Fahad raises an issue regarding an item in the graphical interface as specified in the Software Requirements Specification (SRS). Margaret indicates she has a meeting with the customer at 2:00 and will address the question. With no other concerns raised, the group disperses to their work areas. Panitee reminds Bashar and Jim that there is a detailed design inspection of Fran's inventory order projection module at 1:00.

9:00–10:30   Fran finishes the unit test development on her module design in preparation for the inspection this afternoon. Her design is based on the Software Requirements Specification developed following the tailored REQ script earlier in the project.

Jim begins a personal code review on the inventory status reporting module he finished coding yesterday. He knows from his personal review history that he typically injects 27 coding defects per KSLOC and that in his code reviews he removes about 6 defects per hour. This morning he plans to spend one hour on the review. As he starts, he logs into the time-tracking system and indicates the activity he is working on. Jim reads through the code multiple times, each time looking for a different kind of defect, using a checklist of defect types.

The phone rings and he changes the mode in the time-tracking system. After conferring with his wife on the weekend's activities, he changes the mode back to code review. When he is confident he's found and corrected all the defects that he can and that the number is sufficiently close to his target, he again changes the mode on the time-tracking system, compiles the module, fixes any compilation errors, and begins using the test procedures he developed to make sure the module behaves properly. He logs all the defects he finds according to whether they were found in review, compilation, or test so he can maintain his personal defect rates as well as support project-wide tracking.

Bashar works with the corporate IT staff to resolve an issue with the automated configuration management system. He uses a TSP manual form for recording his time distribution in minutes, including breaks.

Jan attends a divisional strategic planning meeting.

Panitee reviews the current component data collected against the team quality plan to make sure the modules completed are of sufficient quality to be added to the baseline. She uses the automated data collection tool to check the relationship between time coding and time designing, time reviewing and time designing and coding, defects found in review against those found in compiling, defect discovery rate, and review rate. The tool produces a component quality profile (see Figure 3-2), which Panitee uses to identify any questionable work. No modules were identified as problematic, so no decisions need to be made as to how to proceed. Overall, at this point in the development, all the metrics seem in line with those projected, except for the review rate, which has been consistently higher than the planned 200 lines of code per hour. Given that the defect detection yield has not decreased, this is not seen to be a problem.

Greg and Jan begin preparations for the relaunch workshop for the next cycle of the project. They compare the actual progress against the

11:00–12:30

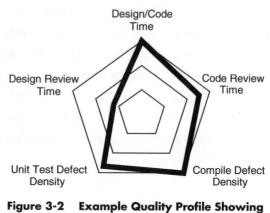

**Figure 3-2 Example Quality Profile Showing
Anomalous Design Review Time**[2]

original launch plan, noting any significant deviations that have occurred since that time and how they might impact the next cycle. It is clear that at least one module that was slated for completion in this cycle won't be ready, but there are two others that actually came in under the estimates and so some work has begun on modules originally slated for the next cycle.

The other team members continue working, making sure they log the time spent on their various project tasks as well as interruptions to their work due to responding to e-mail, phone calls, meetings, breaks, and such. So far the average time spent on project tasks has been around 18 hours per week per person—slightly lower than their initial projections.

1:00–4:30   Panitee conducts the detailed design inspection of Fran's inventory order projection module according to the TSP script (see Figure 3-3 for the TSPi inspection script as an example). Fran, Jim, and Bashar support Panitee in the inspection. They follow a formal inspection process, and data is collected on the number and severity of defects found, time spent, and the size of the module. The inspection rate as well as an

Purpose	To help engineers produce quality products
General	• The purpose of inspections is to focus on sophisticated issues and not on finding simple defects or fixing defects. • Even a few simple defects can distract reviewers so that they are more likely to miss sophisticated problems.
Entry Criteria	A completed and reviewed product with available materials

Step	Activities	Description
1	Plan the Inspection	The producer (or developer) • Arranges with the quality/process manager or some other qualified team member to be the inspection moderator • Handles the mechanics of setting up and running the inspection The moderator (usually the quality/process manager) • Reviews the product to ensure it is ready for the inspection • If not, has the producer fix the problems before proceeding • Selects the other inspection members
2	Hold the Inspection Briefing	The moderator describes the inspection process. The producer familiarizes the inspection team with the product. The reviewers select viewpoints or areas for product concentration. • Sample viewpoints are operation, recovery, maintenance, security, installation, size, and performance. In design inspections, the reviewers also ensure that • At least one reviewer will verify each segment of the design • At least one reviewer will use trace table and/or state machine analysis on every design segment The moderator sets the date and time for the inspection meeting.
3	Review the Product	• The reviewers separately make detailed product reviews. • They mark the defects found on the product documentation. • They record their preparation time.
4	Open the Inspection Meeting	The moderator opens the inspection meeting and • If any reviewers are not prepared, reschedules the meeting • Outlines the inspection meeting procedure
5	Conduct a Product Walk-through	The moderator steps through the product sections and • Has the reviewers describe every defect found • Enters the major defect data on the INS form • Notes the engineers who found each major defect • The owner (producer) enters the major defects in LOGD

(continued)

Figure 3-3   TSPi Inspection Script[3]

6	Estimate the Remaining Defects	• The moderator estimates the defects remaining in the product after the inspection (form INS instructions). • The moderator determines the reviewers' personal yields. • The reviewers note any items to add to their review checklists.
7	Conclude the Inspection Meeting	The inspection team decides • Whether a reinspection is warranted, who should do it, and when • How to verify the defect corrections The moderator completes forms LOGD and INS.
8	Rework the Product and Verify the Fixes	The producer • Makes repairs and updates the product documentation • Holds needed rereviews and/or reinspections • Has the fixes verified as the reviewers recommended in step 7
Exit Criteria		• INS and LOGD forms completed and filed in the project notebook • A fully inspected, high-quality product

Figure 3-3 Continued

estimated inspection yield are calculated at the end of the inspection. The team's experience has shown that high inspection yield (the percentage of the overall module defects that were found in an inspection) can significantly reduce time spent in testing. The inspection of Fran's module takes just over three hours to complete with an estimated yield of 64 percent, which is slightly better than the 61 percent average inspection yield for the project to this point.

2:00–3:00   Margaret meets with the customer representative to update the status of the project. She raises Fahad's issue regarding the user interface and is told she'll have an answer on Monday. Since this will not impact the schedule, she agrees.

3:00–4:00   The team members not involved in the design inspection meet to discuss the integration testing, which will begin next week. As the Testing Manager, Felipe leads the discussions and tasking, with help from

Fahad and Greg. They discuss what strategy to employ in the integration, given their current status and the experience so far in the cycle. Integration testing will show that all necessary components are present and that the interfaces between them work as specified. They identify two units that still need to satisfy their unit test completion criteria and flag this for management attention.

The team ends the week by completing and discussing the weekly status reports and establishing the earned value status for the project. The reports include a Role Report, Risk Report, and Goal Report. Earned value is tracked based on the responsible engineer's estimates for task completion as well as a top-down allocation by the Team Leader and the Planning Manager. Today, the cumulative earned value is 33.74 percent compared to a planned value of 34.5 percent, validating Greg and Jan's findings regarding progress. The Top 10 risk list is reviewed, and no change is made to the order or thresholds. Margaret shares the results of her discussions with the customer. Felipe brings up the unit test completion issue. The problem is some missing customer validity criteria. Margaret takes an action to work this with the customer representative. Panitee brings up the anomaly in review rate, and the team suggests that she investigate the relationship between the review rate and defect detection yield at the unit level. She agrees to do this. All modules are checked into the CM facility, and the team heads home for the weekend.

4:30–5:30

A Typical Day Using Extreme Programming*
Training
The Cockburn Level 2 team leader (coach) and one of the senior programmers attended a 40-hour XP development workshop. Two of the senior programmers had been on an XP team before. One is a Level 2,

Training is both formal and hands-on

*Thanks to Dr. Laurie Williams of North Carolina State University for her help in developing this section.

the other is a strong Level 1A. The remainder of the nine-person team are junior Level 1As who were introduced to the concept through in-house presentations by an XP consultant, enhanced by books and papers suggested by the XP-experienced team members. However, an essential part of the training is done when each of the seven inexperienced team members works side-by-side with one of the trained and/or experienced team members. Two team members are familiar with the legacy system; the others have all reviewed parts of the legacy documentation. The environment ensures that the experts are within earshot of the inexperienced team members. In this way, their experiences are shared (and tacit knowledge is transferred) through their normal work activities. "Default" roles have been established for the team members, as shown in Table 3-2. However, all the team members are always ready to assume other roles within the team in order to get the job done.

Tools and Environment

Space and tools encourage collaboration

The team is using an automated tool to support test case and test suite development. The development space is an open bullpen where all of the team members work and where everyone can respond immediately to questions or calls for help. Workstations are set up in the bullpen to support pair programming, but have been occasionally rearranged when different configurations are needed. Wall space around the bullpen provides white boards and bulletin boards. Areas for phone calls and private time are provided on the periphery. A lounge room with refreshments and comfortable furniture is available for informal discussions and relaxation.

Project Planning

Planning determines the shape and estimated velocity of the project

A one-day exploration session was held with the customer, and the fundamental stories needed for planning were captured on story cards. A two-day planning session was then conducted to allow the customer to refine and prioritize the work to be done based on the developers'

Table 3-2 XP Roles		
Person	**Role**	**Responsibilities**
Jill	Coach	Responsible for the process as a whole. Supports programmers. Maintains stability, depth of understanding of XP. Nudges rather than directs. Separates technical from business decisions.
Melissa	Customer	Responsible for writing and prioritizing stories, making decisions about how to resolve problems, developing functional tests, representing the various user departments' interests.
Ferdinand	Tester	Helps the customer choose and write functional tests; supports programmers in running their tests.
Patricia	Tracker	"Conscience" of the team. Ensures validity of estimates, checks that the velocity is maintained, and acts as historian.
Ford, Gary, Ben, John, Felicity	Programmer	Main player in XP. Responsible for selecting, estimating, and completing tasks; developing unit tests; pair programming; refactoring.

estimate of the resource effort required for implementing the stories. The result of this iterative work determined the iteration length (two weeks), the release length (three iterations), and the release schedule. The workshop also derived an estimate of project velocity (the number of reasonably equal-size stories that can be done in an iteration). Based on the customer priorities, the developer resource estimates, and this velocity, the iteration plan is developed by the developer team and the customer. At the start of each two-week iteration, the programmers select which user stories to own (any left over are assigned). Tasks (which break down the work elements of the stories) are then established from the stories and are described on task cards.

Status

Nearing the second release

The project's second release is due the end of next week, the project having been through five and a half iteration cycles. The first release was deployed with two less stories than originally planned due to the predictable overestimate of project velocity in the first two iterations. One of those stories is included in the current release and the other has been deferred to the next release. Customer feedback has been generally positive, leading to increased clamor for complete functionality.

The Day's Activities

8:30

The team begins the day (as they do every day) with a standup meeting. The whole team stands in a circle. Going around the circle, each person reports specifics on what they accomplished the prior day, any problems they encountered, and what they plan to accomplish today. As they go around the circle, Ford has a question about part of the user interface and sets up a time with Melissa to work the issue. Felicity has a concern about the estimate for her communications utility task, and Ferdinand says he'll take a look at it with her. John asks Gary to work with him on his task to add functionality to the inventory report generator since Gary and Ford did the original development of the functionality. Other pairs form according to the current needs. Jill asks if anyone sees any showstoppers for the planned release. With none identified, the developer pairs settle at workstations to begin the day's work.

9:00–10:30

Gary and John sit at the workstation to enhance the report generator functionality according to the story card and the task description (see Figure 3-4). Initially, John "drives" the workstation and Gary "navigates" as John begins developing test cases for the enhancements. Gary points out some reuse opportunities from the test cases he and Ford developed. He takes over the keyboard and pulls them up to modify them for this new task. The pair work the rest of the morning synchronizing

---

> ### *User Story 15.5*
>
> **Generate a report that compares historical inventory for four previous quarters with current inventory and projected inventory for next two quarters.**
> **User selects "All" or "Select from List" to identify inventory items for report. Allow user to print or view report. Allow user to change inventory item selections.**
> *One day*

> ### *Task Description 15.5-1*
>
> **Identify organization and current date; display screen to get "all" or "select from list" request. If "select from list" display current inventory items, accept multiple picks, and build pick list object. If "all" then build pick list object from current inventory items. Pass pick list object to reporting method.**

Figure 3-4   Story Card and Task Description

breaks and iterating between test case generation and code implementation on a minute-by-minute basis, using the automated test tool to make sure the tests pass consistency and compatibility checks with respect to the rest of the project tests.

Ford and Melissa sit in the lounge to discuss Ford's user interface questions. Melissa lets Ford know that the story doesn't quite fit what they need now, and that's why it may be confusing. She explains what the users need to see to be most effective. Ford takes notes on the story card. Melissa agrees to his suggestion of a quick mockup, and they schedule a meeting after lunch to show her what he's done. Melissa agrees to bring along one of the report users who had a different interpretation of the story. Ford then moves to a free workstation to develop some prototype screens.

Jill meets with her boss to make sure the completion bonus funding is available and that the consultant she wanted to support planning on the next release will be available at the right time.

11:00–12:30   Ferdinand and Felicity meet to discuss the estimate for her communication utility. When Ferdinand looks at the task card for Felicity's story he is not certain exactly which of the target platform's system functions would be the most appropriate. He suggests that they perform a spike to resolve the problem. A spike is a narrow but deep coding experiment that allows the developers to see how various functions might work and to better estimate both system performance and the difficulty of the coding. Felicity agrees and she begins looking at options for the spike.

Ben has asked Jill to help him with his parsing task. As they sit at the workstation, Jill suggests that the new capability enhancements won't fit easily into the existing code. So together they begin to refactor the initial code to remove some redundancy and provide a better design for adding the enhancements.

1:30–3:00   Melissa and Ferdinand begin to finalize the acceptance tests for the current iteration. Because the functionality in this release is more complex than the first release, the tests are more complicated. Ferdinand helps to organize the stories in a way that helps Melissa to develop scenarios that are closer to the way her organization does business and that will cover all of the activities involved in using the new functions. They also refine the approach for stress testing and the always appropriate "Can my 6-year-old break it?" test for unanticipated inputs or sequences. Patricia, as her role as tracker, both participates in and takes notes for the meeting. When the tests are run, she'll collect from the developers the defects found and who's responsible for correction, as well as the new test cases that will be generated to test for those defects in future releases.

John and Gary code their changes, working at the terminal, but breaking a couple of times for snacks and to answer questions from Felicity regarding her spike effort.

Ben and Jill continue their refactoring.

3:30–5:00

Ford and Melissa and the report user grab a workstation and Ford presents his prototype screens. Melissa and the user make some small suggestions (and one pretty big one). Ford counters with an easier but similar suggestion that can be done within the current schedule. The user agrees, but asks that a new story be written to capture the enhancement she wanted for a later iteration. Melissa agrees to coordinate the change with the other report users. Ford decides to get John to pair with him on the implementation of his prototypes on Monday.

John and Gary finish their code and make sure all the unit tests run correctly. Corrections are made until the code passes all of their tests.

5:00–5:30

The team migrates into the lounge area for a wrapup of the day and the week. Progress is reported (and dutifully captured by Patricia) on the various tasks. Patricia then states that according to her data, the project velocity is satisfactory; the team is a little behind schedule, but will not need to renegotiate stories for this iteration. She has updated the schedule and task chart on the wall with her new data. Felicity reports on the findings from her spike, since other tasks will be facing the same problem. Jill congratulates all on a great week, reminds everyone of the postrelease party on next Saturday night after the official installation and acceptance of the new release, and tells everyone to hit the road and have a great weekend.

Crisis Days

Nontypical days

All right, you may say, so far so good. But what happens when the other shoe drops and the manager's nightmare comes true, and the day you thought was typical becomes anything but? Well, let's revisit our hard-working teams and look how each handles a project crisis.

Major change, due in five days

One Friday, unexpectedly, the customer informs the team that there has been a major change in the requirements—the new CEO has requested an unprecedented, complex report to be generated. On inspection, it is discovered that changes will have to be made to the data input GUI, the database, two computational modules, the output GUI, and the hard-copy report generator. To make matters worse, the report is needed for a board of directors meeting the next Wednesday.

A Crisis Day with PSP/TSP

9:00

The customer informs the team of the requirements change and its priority and schedule. She expresses her confidence that the team's track record indicates the change is workable and promises to help expedite any needs they have.

This type of change is anticipated in the architecture, but considerable changes are required in the specs and plans. Assignments are made to estimate the team's ability to complete the change in the requested time.

The team is scheduled to reassemble at 1:00 to decide on its response and to take whatever actions are required.

The team meets and reviews the estimates. Based on current productivity numbers, the team agrees it can meet the deadline, but that there will be considerable impact to the schedule for the next planned release. The replanning effort is completed, the customer informed of the results, and the customer agrees to postpone the next release by the specified time period. Assignments are made and the design tasks begin.

1:00

The team reconvenes to address issues raised in the redesign. The architecture has proven robust and the design work has gone smoothly, aided by automated planning and the use of the Unified Modeling Language (UML) and CM tools, as well as the team's experience with the processes. While there are some grumbles about the hassle of changing the schedule and refocusing their tasks, the prospective satisfaction of fulfilling a CEO-level request and the schedule readjustment leave them enthusiastic. Although their documentation is relatively lightweight, a good deal of rework remains in the plans, earned value system, and test plans and procedures, but some team members with free time on the weekend volunteer to come in and work these. Panitee schedules an inspection meeting Monday afternoon to review the completeness and consistency of the changes.

5:00

The PSP/TSP team could have had significantly more problems had they had:

- A less collaborative and authorized customer.
- An inexperienced manager.
- Weaker tool support.
- A larger change that would have required more cost and schedule adjustment.

A Crisis Day with XP

9:00   The customer informs the team of the requirements change and its priority and schedule at the standup meeting. The team works out its replanning strategy together. Members identify the main contributors to affected modules to write and estimate the tasks.

10:30   The team reconvenes to discuss the results of the task estimation work. Considerable refactoring may be required for the database and report writer modules, but the remainder of the changes look straightforward. The team agrees that they can make the date, but that the time spent will require renegotiating the story content of the current release. The customer works as part of the team to evaluate the options and agrees to push two of the lower-priority stories to the next iteration.

11:00   Pair work begins on writing module tests for the new features. Melissa and Ferdinand sketch out the acceptance test.

1:00   Most of the pairs have finished their initial work. As they make changes to existing software, they use the results from the automated testing suite to identify any errors caused by those changes that have propagated to other parts of the system. The team responsible for the database refactoring realizes that it is proving harder than expected and asks for help. Jill responds and looks at their progress. She sees a way to reuse a pattern from a previous database development she has worked and the refactoring continues more productively. Some problems crop up, though, in undoing the partially completed now-deferred stories and reachieving a simple design.

5:00   The team gathers to take stock. The change has re-energized the team, and Patricia indicates the velocity numbers are significantly higher than they have been for several weeks. It is agreed that they will be able to finish the work within schedule even with the need to rebaseline the design and code. With virtually no paperwork to clean up, the team takes off for the weekend.

The XP team could have had significantly more problems had they had:

- A non-CRACK customer
- A less experienced coach
- A main contributor to one of the affected modules out of the office
- A nonexistent or incomplete set of automated tests
- A larger change that required more impact on the increment contents than the customer could accept within the fixed increment length

Summary

The examples in this chapter are simplified and can only be read as representative of the use of the methods. However, even in this context one can make observations about their use. While they point out the differences between the methods, they also illustrate some strong similarities. These similarities point to some fundamental principles that can form the foundation for hybrid methods.

Even in simplified examples, comparison is possible

Differences

The two approaches have significantly different ideas of the depth and scope of metrics needed to manage the project. TSP has detailed process-control metrics as well as quality and performance measures. The XP measures tend to be product oriented and are used primarily to estimate progress and schedule future iterations.

Depth and scope of metrics

Specificity of process

There is a marked difference between XP and TSP in the specificity of the process followed. XP has a few guidelines and some fairly strict practices, while TSP provides a larger number of detailed scripts, forms, and roles, as well as process exit criteria that serve as baselines for tailoring the project's processes.

Level and scope of reporting

The level and scope of project reporting is another activity where the two approaches vary. XP reporting is generally informal and temporal, while TSP has established reports for many of the tasks and phases of the project that are maintained as a history of the project. XP does have a historian, but the XP notion of history is more one of capturing what did and didn't work rather than documenting activity.

Customer interface

Finally, there is a distinct difference in the way the two approaches handle their customer interface. TSP has a much more formal relationship with the customer than XP's collocated, customer participation paradigm. While both seek support from the customer and are committed to satisfy their needs, there is a contractual feel to the TSP customer relationship, as opposed to the collegial feel in XP.

Similarities

Collaborative teams, well-defined roles, spiral risk- and increment-driven, measurement, test-first

Surprisingly, there are strong similarities in the two methods. Both rely heavily on a collaborative team environment with specific responsibilities, roles, and accountability. There are well-defined roles in each method, although the level of specificity of a particular role differs significantly. Following the spiral philosophy, they are both risk- and increment-driven with iterative planning and execution cycles. Both methods do rely on differing levels of performance measurement to support effort estimation. There is a similar emphasis on technical matters. Test-first is espoused by both of the methods, although XP has a stronger requirement for automated test facilities.

Observations

By observing the nature of the interactions and the type of activities performed in implementing both an agile and disciplined method, it is much easier to see the connection points where the methods may be complementary. In Chapters 4 and 5 we will examine how to take advantage of the similarities to develop successful development strategies.

There are connection points

The bottom line, however, is that getting the people factors right is much more important in the end than technology or method considerations. Each method enabled the team to jell around its mode of operation and to find roles for team members that fit their skills and stimulate their growth. It is likely that some or most of the TSP people would be less than satisfied working on the XP team and vice versa. But diversity is what makes life interesting.

People factors outweigh technical issues

Perhaps the most important people factor in both PSP/TSP and XP is what Watts Humphrey might call "preparedness" and what Kent Beck calls "courage." When PSP/TSP and XP teams are faced with an unanticipated user need, they are quick to respond. They are also quick to prepare and courageously defend a counterproposal for deferring either the previously planned schedule or functionality. Any technique that promotes this kind of preparedness, courage, and solidarity in managing the expectations of overdemanding users has in one stroke removed a major source of software overruns and failures.

Both support pushing back against unreasonable demands

4

Expanding the Home Grounds:
Two Case Studies

Sometimes you just have to see something to believe it can be done.

While the last chapter illustrated the "pure" application of agile and plan-driven methods, it raised the question of what to do on a specific project that may not fit within the conceptual home ground of either approach. Is it really feasible to use a combination of agile and plan-driven methods on future projects? We believe so, and in this chapter summarize two well-documented experiences that illustrate moving the methods away from their home ground. The first describes how leading agile practitioners are using plan-driven techniques to scale up agile methods, and the second, how leading plan-driven practitioners have used agility to streamline their traditional methods.

We look at how the approaches can be altered or enhanced

Using Plans to Scale Up Agile Methods: Lease Management Example

"Bad smells" lead to problems and solutions

The first project involves a comprehensive enterprise resource solution for the leasing industry. Our information comes from an excellent experience report, "Recognizing and Responding to 'Bad Smells' in Extreme Programming," written by Amr Elssamadisy and Gregory Schalliol of ThoughtWorks.[1] "Bad smells" are a parental-experience metaphor for indicators that something in the software needs changing.[2] The report extends the metaphor to include smells that indicate something in your plans and processes may need to be fixed as well.

Large project went to XP after traditional development ineffective

The project had spent about three years using standard XP practices to develop a J2EE application involving over 500 KSLOC. It covered over 1,000 story cards addressing the full range of multicustomer leasing business operations and involved about 30 developers and 20 additional participants, mostly domain experts addressing leasing-business issues. The project went to XP after an 18-month traditional software development approach proved ineffective.

Problems based on breakdowns in XP assumptions

Elssamadisy and Schalliol discuss eight bad smells recognized and resolved by the project. At some risk of oversimplifying a very complex situation, we consolidate them into three sets. Each set represents a breakdown in a fundamental XP assumption:

1. The effort to develop or modify a story really does not increase with time and story number.
2. Trusting people to get everything done on time is compatible with fixed schedules and diseconomies of scale.
3. Simple design and YAGNI scale up easily to large projects.

We will discuss the "smells" associated with each of these assumptions and how they were or could have been resolved by incorporating some form of plan-driven elements into the project's practices.

Assumption 1: The Effort to Develop or Modify a Story Does Not Increase with Time and Story Number

XP assumes that the effort to develop or change a story remains flat as the number of stories developed increases. The lease management system required maintaining tacit knowledge of over 1,000 story cards and 500 KSLOC, across a mixed team of 50 developers and customers. This goes well beyond the ability of people to understand and deal with all of the possible interactions among that many stories and objects in their heads. For example, Elssamadisy and Schalliol estimate that changing a lease (for example, moving it to another state) typically involved working with 100 objects. Complicating this situation, the development personnel changed between iterations, thus straining tacit knowledge even further.

Too much information for tacit knowledge

The first bad smell concerning this assumption occurred when it was recognized that the time to develop a story card increased in later iterations, but the length of the iteration stayed the same. This meant that the project needed to subdivide the stories in later increments in order to meet increment schedules.

Effort to develop features increased over time

A second bad smell was that in later iterations, functions would satisfy their individual tests, but would not integrate well with other functions. After trying to fix the problem within the XP practices, the authors concluded:

Functions failed to integrate— needed high-level architecture

> Were we to employ XP again on a similarly complex project, we would insist upon including the development and constant updating of a more traditional picture or

graphic of the overall application as part of the tasks in each iteration. The aim of such an artifact would be to provide guidance for the writing of story cards and their connected functional tests when the elements of the application under development become very complex and interconnected. To be consistent with the iterative flexibility provided by XP, however, this picture, like the functionality it would represent, would have to be susceptible to modification of some degree at every stage of the development process. Such an integrated picture would provide what a high stack of story cards cannot, namely, a guide for insuring that every new story card can be written and tested completely in its relationships to all other stories.

That is, the project needed to grow an as-needed, easy-to-modify, high-level architectural plan along with the XP practices.

Specialized functions strained tacit knowledge and led to architecture breakers

A third bad smell also focused on unit testing/system testing shortfalls, but led to the recognition that system-level planning attention was necessary to cope with complex specialized functions. This is another area in which tacit knowledge is strained, as people tend to focus on the normal use of features. Some experiences at TRW indicated that off-nominal functionality was a major cause of "architecture breakers": the critical 20 percent of the defects causing 80 percent of the cost-to-fix.[3] Early high-level architectural attention can mitigate such architecture breakers.

Assumption 2: Trusting People to Get Everything Done on Time Is Compatible with Fixed Schedules and Diseconomies of Scale

Customers revisited their early acceptance of features

The first smell that identifies a breakdown of this assumption was described as follows:

After product deliveries following early iterations, the customer has no complaints, but during the late iterations, the customer complains about many things from all iterations. The solution says, "The customer must be 'coached' sufficiently to provide honest and substantial feedback from the very beginning of the development process."

In this case, the "customers" were one step removed from the actual end users. They compounded their limitations by doing less homework on the real needs in the early iterations, perhaps because they thought their other customer functions were more important. Putting blind trust in the "customer is always right" adage can be risky if the customer doesn't fully understand and appreciate the end users' needs. A good deal of early coaching is needed to get on-site customers to appreciate and perform the role of end-user representatives. Otherwise, the on-site customers can become examples of the point in Chapter 2 about the main source of tension in agile methods being between collocated and non-collocated customers.

Tension between non-CRACK customer representatives and other non-collocated users

A second smell illustrates one of the likely side effects of fixed schedules and diseconomies of scale: "Everyone says that all the story cards were finished at the proper times, but it still takes 12 more weeks of full-time development effort to deliver a quality application to the customer." This is related to the previous smell, in that there is a large gray area called "integration" in large systems between zero-defect story completion and acceptable system delivery. And there are other gray areas between "zero defects" and "zero defects plus documentation and standards compliance."

Integration wasn't fully accounted for in planning

The recommended solution was to "Create a precise list of tasks that must be completed before the story is considered finished, and then police it regularly and honestly." This conflicts with agile philosophies such as, "Managers in organizations either have a fundamental trust of people or they don't—there is no middle ground," and "Trust people, mistrust communication"[4] (where "communication" presumably includes plans and

More detailed work plans were needed— tension between small teams and large projects

standards). It illustrates the tension between the agile ideal of small teams, where there's always enough time for everybody to talk through gray areas, and large-project practice, where this would just consume too much time, implying more efficient, objective approaches are needed.

Developers had no time to complete "common" tasks that fell between story cards

The third bad smell for this assumption deals with shared responsibility. "Every developer knew that [a complex, special function] needed to be refactored, but they never made the refactoring." Here is another side effect of fixed schedules and diseconomies of scale: "the tragedy of the commons," in which developers have barely enough time to accomplish assigned work and nobody sees to the common need. The more detailed work plans addressed this need.

Assumption 3: Simple Design and YAGNI Scale Up Easily to Large Projects

Simple design led to problems with foreseeable change

On the lease management project, using simple design and YAGNI on clearly needed families of items (e.g., invoice formats) led to yet another bad smell as the developers constantly refactored the invoice-formatting code, but realized that this was creating point solutions and high refactoring costs for numerous future invoice formats to come.

Software development pattern was the answer

There was a clean technical solution to the problem—the application of a factory pattern—and eventually the team adopted it. This saved them a great deal of refactoring rework, but starting with YAGNI required them to throw away a great deal of point-solution, simple-design code.

Pattern also solved test driver proliferation

The final bad smell emerged from a similar problem in test driver preparation. Different tests required similar test drivers reflecting different points in a business object's lifetime. Developing a specialized version of the factory pattern to handle such families of test drivers saved a great deal of time, but again violated simple design.

Agile Methods Scaleup: Summing Up

The extended-XP approach developed for the lease management system has been highly successful. It provides a solid existence proof that XP can be adapted to develop complex, large-scale applications and corroborated the misconceptions and reality about agile methods in Table 2-3:

Adding some additional discipline helped XP to scale up

- Tacit knowledge promotes agility, but has serious scaling problems as the amount of developed software increases.
- Highly talented people are key to recognizing and responding to the need to diverge from standard XP practices.
- YAGNI and simple design are risky when projects are large and change is foreseeable.

The main solution for scaling-up XP was to introduce elements of plan-driven methods:

- High-level architectural plans to provide essential big-picture information.
- More careful definition of milestone completion criteria to avoid "finishing" but not finishing.
- Use of design patterns and architectural solutions rather than simple design to handle foreseeable change.

However, Elssamadisy and Schalliol are careful to point out that these steps are preferably done as necessary within the fabric of XP for projects of this size and degree of dynamism. In such cases, it is risky to bet on up-front architectures and milestone criteria as compared to as-discovered architectures and milestone criteria.

Using Agility to Streamline Plan-Driven Methods: USAF/TRW CCPDS-R Example

Large, military development project

Our second example is the Command Center Processing and Display System Replacement (CCPDS-R), a project to re-engineer the command center aspects of the U.S. early missile warning system. It covered not only the software but also the associated system engineering and computing hardware procurement. The software effort involved over 1 million lines of Ada code, across a family of three related user capabilities. The developer was TRW; the customer was the U.S. Air Force Electronic Systems Center (USAF/ESC); the users were the U.S. Space Command, the U.S. Strategic Command, the U.S. National Command Authority, and all nuclear-capable Commanders in Chief. The core capability was developed on a 48-month fixed-price contract between 1987 and 1991. While this was admittedly long ago in software time, the project closely mirrors current systems being developed in government and the private sector, and so is relevant as an example. Also, since its process model was one of the contributors to the Rational Unified Process (RUP), it provides a good example of a leaner, agile approach to the use of RUP. A more detailed description of the CCPDS-R project is provided in Walker Royce's book, *Software Project Management.*[5]

Project was high-risk and complex

The project had numerous high-risk elements. One was the extremely high dependability requirements for a system of this nature. Others were the ability to re-engineer the sensor interfaces, the commander situation assessment and decision-aid displays, and the critical algorithms in the application. Software infrastructure challenges included distributed processing using Ada tasking and the ability to satisfy critical-decision-window performance requirements. Many of these aspects underwent considerable change during the development process. The project involved 75 software personnel, most of whom had training in Ada programming but had not applied it to real projects.

CCPDS-R used standard Department of Defense (DoD) acquisition procedures, including a fixed-price contract and the documentation-intensive DoD-STD-2167A software development standards. However, by creatively reinterpreting the DoD standards, processes, and contracting mechanisms, USAF/ESC and TRW were able to perform with agility, deliver on budget and on schedule, fully satisfy their users, and receive Air Force awards for outstanding performance.

Project used military software standards

CCPDS-R used innovative and controversial methods, some of which are closely related to the agile concepts. To show how this was possible, the following four sections indicate how the project was able to develop and apply variants of the four value propositions in the Agile Manifesto.

Approach similar to agile

Individuals and Interactions over Processes and Tools: CCPDS-R

The USAF/ESC's CCPDS-R program office contained a number of particularly enlightened and results-oriented acquisition managers. TRW business practices and corporate values emphasized that the best way to succeed was to make winners of the project's customers, users, maintainers, and performers. Thus, the project's focus was on the win-win interactions of individuals and organizations. There was no way to distinguish this from processes and tools other than to reaffirm that the processes and tools were to be adapted to the needs of the individuals and interactions, rather than vice versa. The team had to choose some processes and tools, and unlike Britcher's FAA example, they chose the ones that helped make winners of the stakeholders rather than the ones that got in the way.

Focused on win-win when selecting tools and revamping processes

Tool and process examples

For CCPDS-R, some examples of this were the following:

■ The DoD acquisition standards were acknowledged, but their milestone content was redefined to reflect the stakeholders' success conditions. Automated tools were used to support the verification of the completeness, consistency, and traceability of the software as it was developed from the specifications. These tools were a significant investment chosen to empower the software developers as well as aid the customers.

■ USAF/ESC and TRW agreed that the contract award fee for good performance would not just go into the TRW corporate profit coffers. Instead, a significant part was set aside for individual project performer bonuses. This not only enhanced motivation and teamwork, but made the CCPDS-R project personnel turnover the lowest in TRW large-project history.

■ The architecture of the system was organized around the performers' skill levels. In particular, previous project experience at TRW and elsewhere had shown high risks of having inexperienced personnel deal with concurrency and Ada tasking constructs. For CCPDS-R, the concurrency architecture and Ada tasking parts of the software were done by experienced Ada developers. The junior programmers were given sequential modules to develop, while being trained by TRW in Ada tasking and concurrency skills for the future.

Working Software over Comprehensive Documentation: CCPDS-R

Moved PDR to the right and used working code as basis for review

The usual DoD-STD-2167A Preliminary Design Review (PDR) to review paper documents and briefing charts around Month 6 was replaced by a PDR at Month 14 that demonstrated working software for all the high-risk areas, particularly the network operating system, the message-passing middleware, and the GUI software. To support this, TRW invested significant resources into a package of message-passing middleware that handled much of the Ada tasking and concurrency management, and provided message ports to accommodate the insertion of sequential Ada packages for the various CCPDS-R application capabilities. For early performance validation, simulators of these functions could be inserted and executed to determine system performance and real-time characteristics. Thus, not only software interfaces, but also system performance could be validated prior to code development, and stubs could be written to provide representative module inputs and outputs for unit and integration testing. Simulators of external sensors and communication inputs and outputs were developed in advance to support continuous testing.

Some CCPDS-R customer personnel and their managers still lived in a world in which receipt of properly formatted documents was important. Since the CCPDS-R architecture and code artifacts were machine processable, it was cheaper to generate the desired documentation than to frustrate customer personnel—not an ideal solution, but a pragmatic real-world compromise.

Automatically generated much required documentation

Customer Collaboration over Contract Negotiation: CCPDS-R

The stakeholder win-win approach adopted by the customer did not regard contract negotiation as antithetical to customer collaboration, but as an opportunity to negotiate contractual agreements (e.g., award fee flowdown to project performers), which rewarded collaborative effort. A well-calibrated cost and schedule estimation model, in this case an Ada version of the Constructive Cost Model (Ada COCOMO), was available for CCPDS-R. It was used to help developers, customers, and users better understand how much functional capability could be developed

Used COCOMO for cost and schedule negotiations

within an available budget and schedule, given the personnel, tools, processes, and infrastructure available to the project.

An architecture for reuse saved effort

The Ada COCOMO cost/performance tradeoff analyses also determined and enabled the savings achieved via reuse across the three different installations and user communities. With a YAGNI approach to the three variants, CCPDS-R would have experienced excessive rework problems similar to those of ThoughtWorks in its continuous refactoring of the lease management system.

Responding to Change over Following a Plan: CCPDS-R

Automated plans and specifications easy to change

As the ThoughtWorks project found for invoice processing, following a plan can often be the best way to respond to change—again, to the degree to which change can be anticipated. Since the CCPDS-R plans and specifications were machine processable, the project was able to track progress and change at a very detailed level. This enabled the developers to anticipate potential downstream problems and largely handle them via customer collaboration and early fixes, rather than delayed problem discovery and expensive technical contract-negotiation fixes.

Metrics showed effectiveness of approach

See Appendix E1

A robust set of metrics was employed in tracking progress and identifying possible problems. Figure 4-1 shows one such metrics-tracking result, the cost of making CCPDS-R changes as a function of time[6] (in the figure, "ECP" stands for "Engineering Change Proposal"). This shows that agile plan-driven methods can approximate the results of no-cost refactoring.

For CCPDS-R, the message-passing middleware and modular applications design enabled the project to be highly agile in responding to change, as reflected in the low growth in cost of change shown in

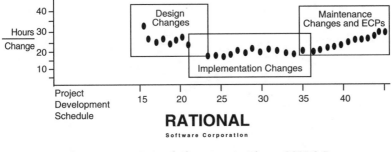

Figure 4-1   Cost of Changes vs. Time: CCPDS-R

Figure 4-1. Further, the project's advance work in determining and planning to accommodate the commonalities and variabilities across the three user communities and installations enabled significant savings in software reuse across the three related CCPDS-R system versions.

Software architecture and design allowed project to respond to changes

Summary

While there are valid concerns about mixing agile and plan-driven processes, our two examples provide existence proofs that the methods can be complementary. The examples also illustrate the necessity of having informed and collaborative stakeholders and project personnel in accomplishing the mix. Figure 4-2 compares the home ground polar graphs for the two projects. The people in these examples succeeded in exchanging a dogmatic mind set for a pragmatic one and determining the best tools and techniques for the project at hand. Table 4-1 is a summary of the misconceptions and observed realities for combining agile and plan-driven methods that complements the counterpart summaries for the individual approaches in Table 2-3.

Examples are existence proofs that hybrids are possible

Now that we know it is possible to overcome the misconceptions and develop hybrid approaches, the stage is set for developing a process to help determine just how and when to attempt this alchemy. Unfortunately,

We need a more general approach

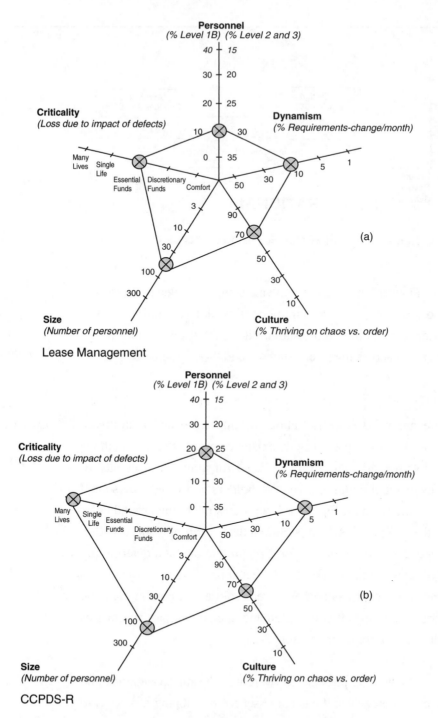

Lease Management

CCPDS-R

Figure 4-2   Home Ground Charts for the Case Studies

Table 4-1 Combining Agile and Plan-Driven Methods: Misconceptions and Reality

Misconception	Reality
Agile and plan-driven methods are completely unmixable.	Agile and plan-driven methods have been successfully combined in a variety of situations.
There are one-size-fits-all process templates for balancing agile and plan-driven methods.	Variations in project risks and stakeholder value propositions lead to different balances of agile and plan-driven methods
Balancing agile and plan-driven methods is a one-dimensional pure- technology, pure-management, or pure-personnel activity.	Balancing agile and plan-driven methods involves multidimensional consideration of technology, management, and personnel factors.

our two examples provide individual solutions rather than guidelines spanning different technology, management, and personnel factors.

Following the method of the lease management example requires that we consider adding discipline to an agile process by recognizing and responding to "bad smells" in the application of the agile methods. This implies that each agile project operating outside the agile home ground needs a relatively scarce Cockburn Level 3 Process Master with enough in-depth understanding of the agile method and the situation to appropriately rebalance the process. Anyone less capable runs the risk of prematurely breaking a workable agile method or of trying to rebalance it in an impractical way. Some of the agilists have recognized this problem and have provided the beginnings of approaches to address it.[7]

Balancing agile and plan-driven methods requires exceptional people

Tools and methods are often misused

The CCPDS-R risk-driven spiral process presented in Royce's book contributed significantly to the development of the Rational Unified Process. However, current RUP guidelines do not address the general problem of balancing agility and discipline. At the 2002 USC agile methods workshop, agilist Alistair Cockburn cited several examples of organizations that interpreted use of the RUP as requiring full compliance with all of the RUP process elements. Rational's Walker Royce responded by saying that these were misuses of the RUP, which is intended to be tailored to different situations. Cockburn commented that this is a common problem with both agile and plan-driven methods—that only about 30 percent of a method's applications are done in the way that the method author intended that they be used. This highlights the importance of having some mechanisms for easily tailoring processes to specific situations; these are currently missing in the RUP package.

5

Using Risk to Balance Agility and Discipline

Getting the formula right entails knowledge, patience, foresight, and communication

The lease management and CCPDS-R case studies in Chapter 4 are particularly good examples of hybrid agile and plan-driven methods that provided different but highly effective balances of agility and discipline to fit their unique situations. However, they do not provide specific guidelines for combining agile and plan-driven methods. In this chapter we offer a way to plan your program and incorporate both agility and discipline in proportion to your project's needs. The criteria we develop are based on your project's particular risks with respect to the use of agile or plan-driven methods. We describe our five-step, risk-based method and then apply it to three related software projects to show how the balance of discipline and agility can change based on project risk patterns.

An Overview of the Method

Five-step process to develop a risk-based strategy

Our method, defined in Table 5-1 and summarized in Figure 5-1, uses risk analysis and a unified process framework to tailor risk-based processes into an overall development strategy. The method relies heavily on the ability of key development team members to understand their environment and organizational capabilities, and to identify and collaborate with the project stakeholders.

Risk analysis to balance too-much or too-little

Risk analysis is used to define and address risks particularly associated with agile and plan-driven methods. It is also used to answer a variety of "How much is enough?" questions by balancing the risks of doing *too little* of something with the risk of doing *too much*. Examples of this approach include answering, "How much prototyping is enough?"[1] and "How much testing is enough?"[2] We extend the approach to consider

Table 5-1 A Tailorable Method for Balancing Agile and Plan-Driven Methods	
Step 1	Rate the project's environmental, agile, and plan-driven risks. If uncertain about ratings, buy information via prototyping, data collection, and analysis.
Step 2a	If agility risks dominate plan-driven risks, go risk-based plan-driven.
Step 2b	If plan-driven risks dominate agility risks, go risk-based agile.
Step 3	If parts of the application satisfy 2a and others 2b, architect the application to encapsulate the agile parts. Go risk-based agile in the agile parts and risk-based plan-driven elsewhere.
Step 4	Establish an overall project strategy by integrating individual risk mitigation plans.
Step 5	Monitor progress and risks/opportunities, readjust balance and process as appropriate.

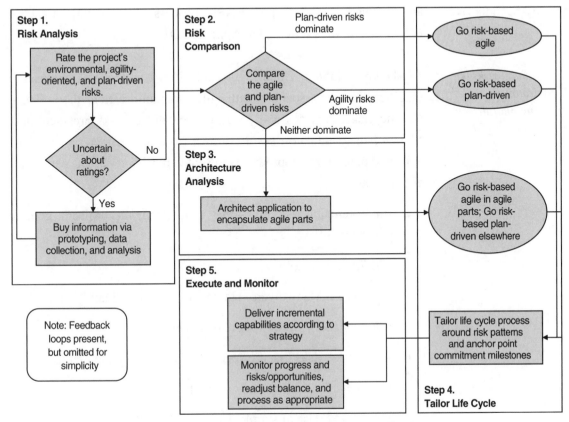

Figure 5-1   Summary of Risk-Based Method

the question, "How much planning and architecting is enough?" as key to balancing agility and discipline.

The process framework is based on the Risk-Based Spiral Model Anchor Points developed by Boehm[3] and the USC Center for Software Engineering affiliated organizations. These anchor points, essentially an integrated set of decision criteria for stakeholder commitment at specific points in the development process, have been adopted by the Rational Unified Process[4] and the Model-Based (System) Architecting

Based on spiral model anchor point milestones

✖ See Appendix D1

and Software Engineering (MBASE) process.[5] More detail on anchor point milestones is provided in Appendix D1.

Candidate risks for environment, agile, and plan-driven

As shown in Table 5-1 and Figure 5-1, Step 1 applies risk analysis to specific risk areas associated with agile and plan-driven methods. Three specific risk categories and associated candidate risks are identified. Many of the candidate risks are drawn from the characteristics of the agile and plan-driven approaches presented in Chapter 2. The categories and risks are

- Environmental risk: risks that result from the project's general environment

  - *E-Tech.* Technology uncertainties

  - *E-Coord.* Many diverse stakeholders to coordinate

  - *E-Cmplx.* Complex system of systems

- Agile risks: risks that are specific to the use of agile methods

  - *A-Scale.* Scalability and criticality

  - *A-YAGNI.* Use of simple design or YAGNI

  - *A-Churn.* Personnel turnover or churn

  - *A-Skill.* Not enough people skilled in agile methods

- Plan-driven risks: risks that are specific to the use of plan-driven methods

  - *P-Change.* Rapid change

  - *P-Speed.* Need for rapid results

  - *P-Emerge.* Emergent requirements

  - *P-Skill.* Not enough people skilled in plan-driven methods

Step 1, while not a simple task, provides the basis for making decisions about the development strategy later in the process. If there is too much uncertainty about some of the risk categories, it is prudent to spend resources to buy information about the project aspects that create the uncertainty. It is important to understand that the candidate risks we describe are just that—candidates for consideration. They are neither complete nor always applicable, but are there as guides to stimulate your thinking. One tool used in this analysis is the risk exposure profile. We will use it extensively in our examples.

Step 1 provides the basis

Step 2 evaluates the results of the risk analysis to determine if the project at hand is appropriate for either purely agile or purely plan-driven methods. This is the case when the project characteristics fall squarely in one or the other approach's home ground as discussed in Chapter 2.

Step 2 looks for a consistent home ground

Step 3 deals with the case where the project has no clear agile or plan-driven home ground or when parts of the system have such different risks that they fall into different home grounds. If possible, an architecture is developed that supports using agile methods where their strengths can be best applied and their risks minimized. Plan-driven methods are used for the remainder of the work and are considered the default where no suitable architecture can be created. Note that this analysis may uncover a new risk or opportunity that requires backtracking to an earlier step. These backtracks are omitted from the figures for simplicity.

Step 3 is for hybrid risks

The focus of Step 4 is developing an overall project strategy that addresses the identified risks. This involves identifying risk resolution strategies for each of the risks and integrating them. The specifics of the process will depend primarily on the developer organization's capabilities and experience in the general application area. A successful and experienced developer will have highly capable people for defining,

Step 4 develops the strategy

designing, developing, and deploying the application. Such a developer could also take advantage of reusable process assets and product patterns in establishing the strategy. A less experienced in-house or external developer must perform additional learning-curve and asset-buildup activities to ensure success. We advocate using the Life Cycle Architecture anchor point milestone criteria as exit criteria from Step 4.

See Appendix D1

Step 5 allows for strategy adjustment

It is important to understand that no decision is perfect or good for all time, and, as indicated in Step 5, the management team needs to constantly monitor and evaluate the performance of its selected processes as well as keep an eye on the environment. This step is similar to the agile practice of "reflection." If your process is generating some "bad smells," you need to backtrack, revalidate, and perhaps adjust the levels of agile or plan-driven methods you initially established. Adjustments should be made as soon as the smells arise. On a more positive note, monitoring can also identify opportunities to improve value to the customer, shorten time-to-delivery capabilities, and improve stakeholder involvement.

An Example Family of Applications: Agent-Based Planning Systems

In order to illustrate the practical application of our risk-based method, we want to establish a realistic context. To do this, we introduce a family of representative current and future software applications. We will show how, for each of three representative systems, the project risks suggest a different mix of agile and plan-driven process components.

Software agents search for and locate information across a network

Agent-based planning systems are good examples of emerging future software applications. They involve the use of software agents to search for and locate desired information across a network; to analyze the information and determine recommended choices (e.g., best-buy recommendations);

to develop plans for implementing a course of action involving the chosen elements (including functions such as dependency analysis and constraint satisfaction); and to monitor the implementation of the plans to identify potential difficulties in realizing the plans.

A number of agent-based planning systems have been successfully developed and used.[6] They can provide significant improvements in operational efficiency, human error reduction, speed of execution, adaptability to changing situations, and support of complex collaborative enterprises.

Agent-based systems provide significant improvements

On the other hand, agent-based systems involve a number of risks, which are still being addressed by research and early applications. These include verification and validation of agent behavior, scalability of multiagent behavior, commonsense reasoning about bad data or unexpected events, and ability to degrade gracefully vs. fail catastrophically.

Agent-based systems have significant risks

Given these characteristics, balancing risks and opportunities is challenging in agent-based systems, with the difficulty varying considerably depending on the scale and criticality of the application. We have seen in Chapter 2 that scale and criticality are also identified as significant risk factors for deploying agile and plan-driven methods.

Agent-based systems are good as examples

Our three representative example applications are

Our three representative systems

1. Small, relatively noncritical: an agent-based planning system for *managing events* such as conferences or conventions (based on the risk patterns observed in small, campus Web services applications).
2. Intermediate: an agent-based planning system for *supply chain management* across a network of producers and consumers (based on the risk patterns discussed in ThoughtWorks' experience scaling up XP to a 50-person project in a lease management application[7]).

3. Very large, highly critical: an agent-based planning system for *national crisis management* (based on risk patterns observed in the U.S. DARPA and U.S. Army Future Combat Systems program—an over-1,000 person, agent-oriented, network-centric system of systems).

Table 5-2 summarizes each application's situation with respect to the major agile/plan-driven home ground characteristics we have discussed earlier.

We start from the middle and work outward

As a first example of our risk-based methodology, since its context is similar to the previously discussed lease management example, we'll address the intermediate application. Using this application as a reference point, we can then see how the risk patterns of the smaller and larger applications determine different balances of agile and plan-driven methods.

An Intermediate Application: Supply Chain Management

Turnkey supply chain management systems for manufacturers

SupplyChain.com is a commercial software house that specializes in developing turnkey agent-based supply chain management systems for, and in collaboration with, large manufacturing companies. These client companies generally have complex networks of suppliers to their manufacturing processes and complex networks of distributors for their manufactured products. SupplyChain.com's experience has made it a leader in this area, but the area is too dynamic and driven by customer-specific considerations (supply-and-demand dynamics, geography and globalization, in-house software compatibility, critical dependencies and timelines) to enable much use of prebuilt plug-and-play application components.

As indicated in Table 5-2, their applications typically involve distributed, multiorganization teams of about 50 people. Their primary objective is to provide a rapid increase in value to the manufacturing company through increases in supply chain speed, dependability, and adaptability. Parts of

Parts of the application are stable, others volatile

Table 5-2 Summary of Example Application Characteristics			
Application	**Event Planning**	**Supply Chain Management**	**National Crisis Management**
Team size	5	50	500
Team type	In-house/ venture startup; collocated	Distributed; often multiorganization	Highly distributed, multiorganization
Failure risks	Venture capital; manual effort	Major business losses	Large loss of life
Clients	Single collocated representative	Multiple success-critical stakeholders	Many success-critical stakeholders
Requirements	Goals generally known; details emergent	Some parts relatively stable, others volatile, emergent	Some parts relatively stable, others volatile, emergent
Architecture	Provided by single COTS package	Mostly provided by small number of COTS packages	System of systems; many COTS packages
Refactoring	Inexpensive with skilled people	More expensive, with mix of people skills	Feasible only within some subsystems
Primary objective	Rapid value	Rapid value increase, dependability, adaptability	Rapid response, safety, security, scalability, adaptability

their applications are relatively stable, while others are highly volatile. Their architectures are driven by a few key COTS packages that are also continually evolving. The risk of system failure involves major business losses.

Agile and plan-driven aspects to the program

Clearly there are agile aspects to the program (i.e., rapid value, volatility) as well as plan-driven aspects (i.e., scalability, criticality). In the following sections we apply the five-step process described in Figure 5-1 to determine an appropriate strategy for the project.

Step 1: SupplyChain.com Project Risk Ratings

Our analysis for balancing agile and plan-driven methods begins by assessing the major sources of environmental, agile, and plan-driven risks.

SupplyChain.com Environmental Risks

Technical and coordination risks

There are significant technical risks. These include the uncertainties cited above for agent-based systems (*E-Tech*) and the existence of many separately evolving networks of suppliers and distributors to be coordinated (*E-Coord*).

SupplyChain.com Agile Risks

Scale and YAGNI risks

The agile risks are similar to those of the lease management system discussed in Chapter 4. Reconciling the inherent diseconomies of scale of a 50-person project with the desire to maintain system dependability across constant increment delivery intervals is difficult (*A-Scale*). In the same way, it will be a challenge to reconcile the desire of agile developers to follow YAGNI and simple design with the knowledge that parts of the application will be stable and would thus benefit from anticipatory architectures (*A-YAGNI*). SupplyChain.com's relatively stable workforce lowers the possibility that turnover of key personnel will disrupt the project's reliance on tacit knowledge (*A-Churn*).

SupplyChain.com Plan-Driven Risks

The plan-driven risks largely involve incurring extensive delays through rework of elaborate plans and specifications in a rapidly evolving, time-critical marketplace. There would probably be slow and expensive adaptation of elaborate plans and specifications to rapid changes in technology, organizations, and market conditions (*P-Change*). The inability to deliver new capabilities rapidly enough to keep pace with the competition can lead to loss of market share (*P-Speed*). Over-reliance on prespecified requirements in areas where requirements may emerge through user familiarization and experience can affect the project architecture and plans in unpredictable ways (*P-Emerge*).

Change speed and emergence risks

Step 2: Compare the Agile and Plan-Driven Risks

In Step 2, we first determine whether the project situation is dominated by agile risks or plan-driven risks. Table 5-3 summarizes the risks based on the above discussion, and Figure 5-2 shows how SupplyChain.com looks on the home ground polar chart.

The primary agile risks of scalability, criticality, and use of simple design can be addressed by selective application of plan-driven planning and architecting techniques in a manner similar to the lease management example in Chapter 4. The combined plan-driven risks of rapid change, need for rapid response, and emerging requirements could be addressed by selective application of agile methods within an overall plan-driven framework. A suitably agile RUP or TSP team could most likely succeed.

Agile and plan-driven risks can be seen and mitigated

Given SupplyChain.com's culture and environment, our decision is to apply a risk-based agile approach. If, however, SupplyChain.com's environment included a more stable, well-understood, financially critical marketplace and a high rate of agile personnel turnover, the risk-based plan-driven approach would be preferable.

We choose a risk-based agile approach

Table 5-3 Risk Ratings for SupplyChain.com	
Risk Items	**Risk Ratings**
Environmental risks	
E-Tech. Technology uncertainties	■■
E-Coord. Many stakeholders	■
E-Cmplx. Complex system of systems	■
Risks of using agile methods	
A-Scale. Scalability and criticality	■■
A-YAGNI. Use of simple design	■■
A-Churn. Personnel turnover	■
A-Skill. Not enough people skilled in agile methods	■
Risks of using plan-driven methods	
P-Change. Rapid change	■■
P-Speed. Need for rapid results	■■
P-Emerge. Emergent requirements	■■
P-Skill. Not enough people skilled in plan-driven methods	■
Risk rating scale: ■■—**Serious but manageable risk**	
□—**Minimal risk** ■■■—**Very serious but manageable risk**	
■—**Moderate risk** ■■■■—**Showstopper risk**	

Need to plan, but how much? With either approach, there is a need to determine the appropriate amount of planning. Different risk patterns can lead to very different decisions. Our tailoring approach in Figure 5.1 involves developing

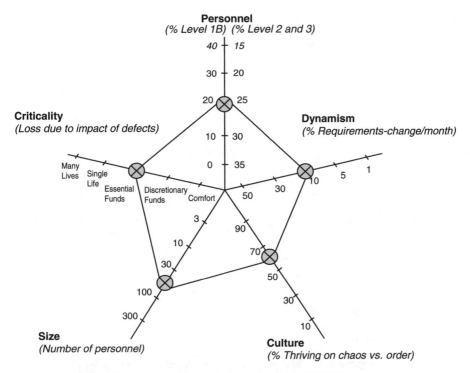

Figure 5-2   Home Ground Chart for SupplyChain.com

strategies for resolving individual risks and integrating the strategies together via the spiral anchor point milestones.

Using Risk to Determine "How Much Planning Is Enough?"

A central concept in risk management is the risk exposure (RE) involved in a given course of action. It is determined by assessing the probability of loss—$P(L)$—involved in a course of action and multiplying it by the corresponding size of loss—$S(L)$: $RE = P(L) \times S(L)$. Loss can include profits, reputation, quality of life, or other value-related attributes.

Risk Exposure = Probability of Loss × Size of Loss

The solid curve in Figure 5-3 shows the variation in risk exposure due to inadequate plans. This is a function of the level of investment that Sup-

Determine the RE for inadequate plans

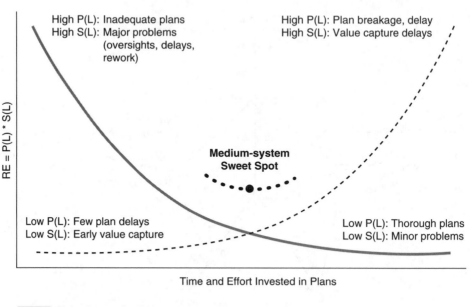

High P(L): Inadequate plans
High S(L): Major problems
(oversights, delays,
rework)

High P(L): Plan breakage, delay
High S(L): Value capture delays

**Medium-system
Sweet Spot**

Low P(L): Few plan delays
Low S(L): Early value capture

Low P(L): Thorough plans
Low S(L): Minor problems

Time and Effort Invested in Plans

——— Risk exposure due to inadequate plans
- - - - Risk exposure due to market share erosion
● ● ● ● Sum of risk exposures

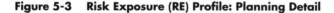

Figure 5-3   Risk Exposure (RE) Profile: Planning Detail

ply Chain.com will put into a project's process and product plans. At the left, a minimal investment corresponds to a high probability that the plans will have loss-causing gaps, ambiguities, and inconsistencies. It also corresponds to a high size of loss because these deficiencies will cause major project oversights, delays, and rework costs—particularly due to agility risks *A-YAGNI* (inadequate architectures for predictable application elements) and *A-Churn* (loss of tacit information due to personnel turnover). At the right, the more thorough the plans, the less probability that plan inadequacies will cause problems and the smaller the size of the associated losses.

The dashed curve shows the variation in RE due to market share erosion through delays in product introduction. Spending little time in planning will get at least an initial capability into the marketplace early, enabling early value capture. Spending too much time in planning will have a high *P(L)* due both to the planning time spent and to rapid changes causing delays via plan breakage—plan-driven risk *P-Change* above. It will also cause a high *S(L)*, as the delays will enable others to capture most of the market share (plan-driven risk *P-Speed*).

Determine the RE for market share erosion over time

The dotted curve shows the sum of the risk exposures due to inadequate plans and market share erosion. It shows that very low and very high investments in plans have high overall risk exposures, and that there is a "sweet spot" in the middle where overall risk exposure is minimized, indicating "How much planning is enough?" for SupplyChain.com's operating profile.

Sum of the REs yields the sweet spot

Step 4a: Individual Risk Resolution Strategies
Given that Step 2 resulted in a risk-based agile decision, Step 3 is bypassed, and the next step is to identify a resolution strategy for each risk (Step 4a).

E-Tech: Technical Uncertainties
One major source of uncertainty is the set of technical risks associated with agent-based systems. Before committing to a specific agent-coordination approach or package, it is important to determine critical agent and agent-coordination objectives, constraints, and priorities, and to use them in evaluating the agent technology candidates via appropriate combinations of reference checking, analysis, benchmarking, and prototyping.

Technology watch and analysis

A similar source of uncertainty is the set of technical risks associated with the performance and interoperability of COTS packages used across the supply chain's stakeholder organizations. Similar risk assessment

COTS watch and analysis

strategies are needed to establish satisfactory combinations of COTS packages. For both of these technical uncertainty areas, a continuing technology-watch activity is needed to assess emerging technology risks and opportunities.

E-Coord, E-Cmplx: Many Separately Evolving Networks of Suppliers and Distributors

Involve the stakeholders

�֍ See Appendix D2

A major risk is to proceed too rapidly without the involvement of success-critical stakeholders. Concentrating on supply chain logistics management without considering financial stakeholders and concerns is an example of such a risk. Techniques such as the DMR Consulting Group's Results Chain[8] are good for identifying missing success-critical initiatives and stakeholders. Involving all success-critical stakeholders in win-win feature prioritization mitigates the risks of win-lose situations, which often become lose-lose.

CRACK representatives are success-critical

Another major risk is to accept unqualified stakeholder representatives as team members. Busy stakeholder organizations will be tempted to assign representatives whose presence won't be missed—particularly if a full-time representative is required. SupplyChain.com has seen the unfortunate results and is able to convince such organizations that they don't want to repeat them. Stakeholder representatives should be CRACK performers: Collaborative, Representative, Authorized, Committed, and Knowledgeable. Shortfalls in any of these capabilities can lead to frustration, delay, and wasted project effort, not to mention a nonacceptable product. It is better to get a part-time CRACK performer than a full-time non-CRACK performer.

Negotiate and document interfaces

A third major risk is the difficulty of coordinating interface protocols among dynamically evolving networks of suppliers and distributors with different internal evolution strategies. It requires considerable up-front work to establish mutual commitments to relatively stable interface protocols, with continuing work to monitor and evolve mutually satisfactory changes.

A-Scale: Diseconomies of Scale

Almost all of the agilists with whom we have discussed this issue blanch at the idea of lengthening the release interval as the application gets larger and as the effort required to develop and integrate new stories increases. But something needs to be done to avoid the types of bad smells encountered in the lease management application and similar large agile projects.

Variable iteration lengths may be appropriate

One approach that may enable conserving the release interval is to make later stories more granular and amenable to timeboxing. However, in larger, multiteam applications, this requires further coordination to ensure that one team's dropped features are not needed by another team's application component.

Timeboxing can stabilize the release interval

A-YAGNI: Foreseeable Change vs. YAGNI and Simple Design

As with the lease management application, the supply chain application will have some foreseeable sources of change, such as new data and operations involved in supply chain transactions. And as with the lease management application, factory patterns or other change-prescient architecture techniques can be used to create a framework for accommodating such sources of future change much more readily than with simple design and continuous refactoring. A good method for change-prescient architecture development is the information-hiding technique of encapsulating foreseeable sources of change within individual modules,[9] thus eliminating the ripple effects caused by such changes.

Architecture and design patterns accommodate foreseeable change

A-Churn: Loss of Tacit Knowledge via Personnel Turnover

Alternate representatives and completion bonuses stabilize teams

Within the development team, tacit knowledge losses can be reduced by rotating people across programming pairs or across feature teams. Equally critical are losses of key supply chain stakeholder representatives: Keeping alternate representatives involved can reduce the impact of such losses. As with the CCPDS-R example, SupplyChain.com and its operational stakeholders can reduce the probability of loss as well as the size of loss due to personnel turnover by establishing significant bonuses for successful project completion.

P-Change, P-Speed, P-Emerge: Delays and Reduced Competitiveness via Reliance on Elaborate Prespecified Plans and Specifications

Agile methods address the plan-driven risks

The use of agile methods addresses these risks. Rapid change is addressed by short iterations and a balance of simple design and change-prescient architecture. Rapid results are addressed by short iterations and pair programming. Emergent requirements are addressed by short iterations and dedicated CRACK customer representatives.

Risk-based specifications avoid excessive documentation

An effective approach to overspecification risks is the use of risk-based specifications:[10]

- *Don't* write specifications when the risk of *not* using them is low and the risk of *using* them is high. A good example is a written specification of the GUIs. With a good GUI-builder tool, the risk of not writing specifications is low. With extensive GUI iteration, the risk of expensive specification rework is high.
- *Do* write specifications when the risk of *using* them is low and the risk of *not* using them is high. A good example is a written specification of the results of extensive stakeholders' negotiations on supply chain interface protocols.

A similar approach can be applied for risk-based process plans. For the various organizations making commitments to the timing of introducing new operational interfaces and business workflows, it would be risky not to develop top-level milestone plans and critical-path dependencies. On the other hand, with an experienced team and rapidly changing circumstances, use of a detailed earned value management system would add more risk of delay than it would subtract.

Risk-based processes avoid excessive bureaucracy

Risk-based testing is another area in which a bit of planning can save downstream time and effort. Most projects spend as much time and effort on testing the low-risk parts of the code as on the high-risk parts. Focusing the test effort on the high-risk parts—agent coordination, potentially critical failure modes, highest-value business workflows—can not only generate project time and effort savings, but also avoid high-cost operational losses.

Risk-based testing avoids low-value test effort

Step 4b: Risk-Based Strategy for SupplyChain.com System Development

Figure 5-4 and Table 5-4 summarize an overall project strategy that integrates the individual risk resolution approaches discussed above. The figure describes participant groups by horizontal swim lanes, with the project activities in rectangles overlaying lanes of the participant groups involved. The figure identifies phases with shaded areas, and decision points (the spiral anchor point milestones) with ovals. In this case, there are three primary participant groups:

Three major participant groups are success-critical

- *A group of operational stakeholders.* These include a largely dedicated manufacturing company representative, a part-time supplier company representative, and a part-time distributor company representative. Each are CRACK performers. They have alternates who ensure continuity of representation and also call on as-needed specialists from other parts of the organizations that they represent.

■ *A risk/opportunity management team.* The SupplyChain.com project manager and three senior (Cockburn Level 2 or 3) Supply-Chain.com staff members form a risk/opportunity management team. These members maintain a continuous watch for emerging project risks or opportunities. When such risks or opportunities arise, the risk management team initiates actions (e.g., prototyping, COTS evaluation, change proposal evaluation, complex refactoring) to explore options and to develop an appropriate response to the risk or opportunity. When no major risks or opportunities are active, they contribute to one of the development teams—often in a mentoring role. They should have both agile and plan-driven method skills to ensure balance.

■ *A group of agile feature teams.* These operate concurrently to develop the features involved in each increment of system capability. The teams are primarily focused on particular application areas (e.g., supplier transactions, distributor transactions, manufacturing support). Their team leaders are Cockburn Level 2 personnel. The team members are mixes of Level 2 and Level 1A personnel. There are no Level 1B personnel. Personnel will rotate across teams. There will be a ramp-up of team members coming from the manufacturing company since it will eventually take over continuing software development.

Three-phase strategy: Phase 1 = Inception

The risk patterns for projects of this scale and complexity make it best to organize the projects into three primary phases. Phase 1, roughly corresponding to a RUP/MBASE Inception phase, involves rapid team-building and development of a shared system vision among the stakeholders (the feature teams are represented by their team leaders in the first two phases). Example techniques used in this phase are proto-

Table 5-4 SupplyChain.com Risk Mitigation Strategies

Risk Items	Mitigation Approaches
Environmental risks	
E-Tech. Technology uncertainties	Risk-driven technology prototypes; Technology and COTS watch
E-Coord. Many stakeholders	Results chain; Stakeholder win-win; CRACK representatives
E-Cmplx. Complex system of systems	Architecture determination; Early commitments on validated interfaces
Risks of using agile methods	
A-Scale. Scalability and criticality	Subsettable stories; Longer iterations as size/complexity grows
A-YAGNI. Use of simple design	Balance with high-level change-prescient architecture; Design patterns
A-Churn. Personnel turnover	Personnel backups; Pair programming; Project completion bonuses
A-Skill. Not enough people skilled in agile methods	Low-risk
Risks of using plan-driven methods	
P-Change. Rapid change	Short iterations; Balanced simple design and change-prescient architecture
P-Speed. Need for rapid results	Short iterations; Pair programming; Timeboxing
P-Emerge. Emergent requirements	Short iterations; Dedicated customer
P-Skill. Not enough people skilled in plan-driven methods	Risk management team with agile and plan-driven method skills

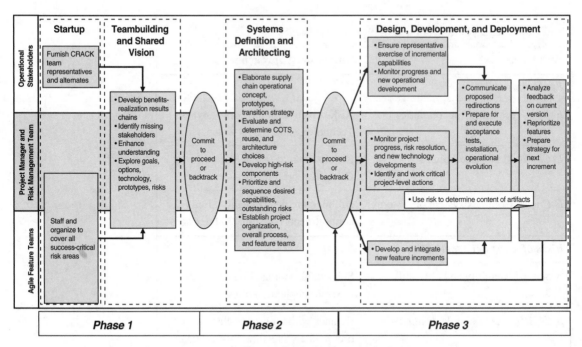

Figure 5-4   Overall SupplyChain.com Project Strategy

typing key user features, COTS evaluation, brainstorming, results chain development, and negotiation of a mutually satisfactory set of strategic project objectives and priorities.

Phase 2 =
Elaboration

Phase 2, roughly corresponding to a RUP/MBASE Elaboration phase, establishes the overall operational concept and life cycle strategy; a set of key COTS, reuse, and architecture decisions, including development of high-risk components; a full project organization; and an initial set of top-priority features to develop in Increment 1. Both Phase 1 and Phase 2 are concluded by a successful review by senior experts and stakeholder representatives, and by full stakeholder commitment to support the next phase (or not, in which case the project is terminated or backtracked to Phase 1 or earlier activities of Phase 2).

In situations involving

*Possible to combine
Phases 1 and 2*

- well-jelled, domain-experienced developers with over 40 percent Cockburn Level 2 and 3 people;
- well-jelled, CRACK customers with a clear set of business objectives; and
- mature domain architectures and COTS products

the activities in Phases 1 and 2 can be combined and completed in a week. If most of these conditions are not true, a better estimate would be three months each for Phases 1 and 2.

In Phase 3, the feature teams develop successive increments of prioritized system capability in parallel. The operational stakeholders ensure that each increment is exercised and iterated based on feedback from representative users. The entire team collaborates to surface and deal with emerging risks and opportunities, make and evaluate change proposals, and support each increment's transition into operational use. A final shared task is to prepare the strategy for the next increment, consolidating lessons learned, planning for process improvement, and perhaps backtracking to earlier phases.

*Phase 3 implements
the system
incrementally*

Small Application: Event Planning

Rapid Value is a small startup company formed by former Supply-Chain.com employees who preferred a diverse set of smaller agent-based planning applications to a repetitive stream of larger supply chain applications. They have created a set of agent-based packages that extend standard COTS business software packages for planning, scheduling, and coordinating, along with associated publishing, financial, and logistics management support.

*Spin-off from
SupplyChain.com*

Event planning application

Their next project is an agent-based event planning application for Event Managers, Inc. The typical Event Managers job involves managing the infrastructure and operations of conferences and conventions: facilities, equipment, supplies, communication, information processing, audio-visual, food and beverage, exhibits, special events, VIP handling, transportation, lodging, registration, finance, publications, publicity, and so on.

Work is repetitive, but with wide variations

Much of the event planning work is highly repetitive and can benefit from automation. From one event to the next, however, there is a widening variety of options and interdependencies, which makes an agent-based approach highly attractive. Fortunately, the Event Managers staff is experienced and creative enough to create workarounds for various kinds of event breakdowns, makng the risk of agent-based planning system breakdowns relatively low. Table 5-5 summarizes the characteristics of this small Event Managers application and compares it with the intermediate-sized supply chain management application.

Step 1: Event Planning Project Risk Ratings

Environmental and agile risks low but plan-driven risks high

In comparison with the SupplyChain.com risks, the environmental risks of technology uncertainties such as scalable agent coordination (*E-Tech*) and multiple stakeholders (*E-Coord*) are much lower. The risks of too much agility are also much lower: problems of scale and criticality (*A-Scale*); repetitive refactoring (*A-YAGNI*); disruption of tacit knowledge via personnel turnover (*A-Churn*); and conservation of familiarity with frequent releases. Another agility risk is that none of the current Event Managers employees knows enough about modern information technology to be a CRACK performer (*A-Skill*). However, the plan-driven risks are higher: adaptation of plans to rapid change (*P-Change*); need for rapid results (*P-Speed*); and emergent rather than prespecifiable requirements (*P-Emerge*).

Step 2: Compare the Agile and Plan-Driven Risks

Table 5-5 summarizes the comparison of agile and plan-driven risks with respect to the counterpart SupplyChain.com risk assessment. Event Managers' plan-driven risks are quite high in comparison, leading to a more definitive decision to go risk-based agile. Figure 5-5 shows the home ground polar chart for Event Managers.

Definitely risk-based agile

Planning Risk Exposure Profile

The risk exposure profile for the small Event Managers system has a similar risk exposure for planning delays, but a much lower risk exposure for rework delays. The probability of loss is smaller due to having

Sweet spot moves to left—less planning required

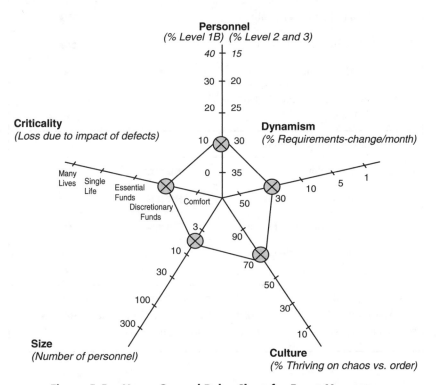

Figure 5-5   Home Ground Polar Chart for Event Managers

e

Table 5-5 Risk Ratings for Event Managers and SupplyChain.com		
Risk Items	**Risk Ratings**	
	Event Managers	**SupplyChain.com**
Environmental risks		
E-Tech. Technology uncertainties	■	■■
E-Coord. Many stakeholders	□	■
E-Cmplx. Complex system of systems	□	■
Risks of using agile methods		
A-Scale. Scalability and criticality	□	■■
A-YAGNI. Use of simple design	□	■■
A-Churn. Personnel turnover	■■	■
A-Skill. Not enough people skilled in agile methods	□	■
Risks of using plan-driven methods		
P-Change. Rapid change	■■■■	■■
P-Speed. Need for rapid results	■■■■	■■
P-Emerge. Emergent requirements	■■■■	■■
P-Skill. Not enough people skilled in plan-driven methods	□	■
Risk rating scale: □—**Minimal risk** ■—**Moderate risk**	■■—**Serious but manageable risk** ■■■—**Very serious but manageable risk** ■■■■—**Showstopper risk**	

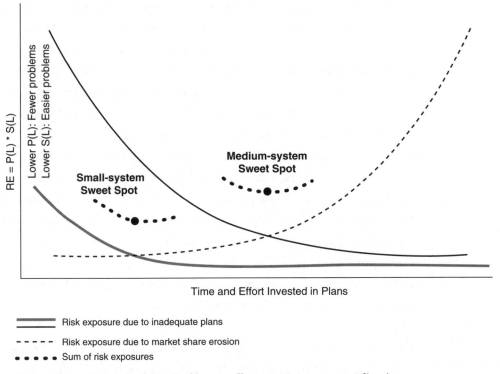

Figure 5-6   Risk Exposure Profile: Small Event Managers Application

fewer problems or sources of risk, and the size of loss is lower as the problems are easier to fix. The resulting small-system sweet spot, as shown in Figure 5-6, moves considerably to the left and down, indicating that the use of agile methods for the event planning application is both low-risk and less risky than even a moderately plan-driven approach.

Steps 4a, 4b: Risk-Based Strategy for Event Planning System Development

The Rapid Value project manager and the Event Managers client representative achieved a shared vision of the project's objectives, scope, and approach in three days. They discussed technical risks, staffing risks,

Collaborative completion of Phase 1

Agile risks are low and manageable

and the risks of doing relatively little vs. very much plan documentation. They agreed that minimal documentation is needed. To address the *A-Skill* risk of a lack of an IT-knowledgeable client representative, and for the transition of the system over to maintenance by Event Managers, both managers agreed that one of the development team members should be a maintenance programmer, to be hired by Event Managers. They jointly reviewed the candidates and selected one with good, related XP experience and considerable interest in the event management business. They performed a short prototyping spike to address the agent coordination technology risks. The risk of personnel turnover in a highly dynamic marketplace was handled by negotiating successful completion bonuses for developers and by using pair programming. They chose a mix of Scrum and XP to minimize the impact of rapid change, rapid results, and emergent requirements. A week later, the team had been formed and had completed Phase 1.

Informal approach in keeping with agile methods

The functions performed in Figure 5-4 for the supply chain application are still important functions for the Event Managers application. Event Managers can use Figure 5-4 as a checklist for early planning, but by following the risk-based content principle at the right of the figure, they converge on an informal approach to the steps and an outcome of shared tacit knowledge rather than documented knowledge. Table 5-6 identifies their selected risk mitigation strategies. The resulting process, shown in Figure 5-7, is a merge of Scrum and XP similar to the XBreed process,[11] or the related XP@Scrum process. Scrum is used to determine the Product Backlog of prioritized capabilities and the high-level architecture (here furnished via Rapid Value's COTS-based framework). The Scrum Sprints are then largely accomplished by using the XP practices. Each XP/Sprint increment is then system tested and transitioned into system operation.

Table 5-6 Event Managers Risk Mitigation Strategies	
Risk Items	**Mitigation Approaches**
Environmental risks	
E-Tech. Technology uncertainties	Agent coordination prototype
E-Coord. Many stakeholders	Low-risk
E-Cmplx. Complex system of systems	Low-risk
Risks of using agile methods	
A-Scale. Scalability and criticality	Low-risk
A-YAGNI. Use of simple design	Low-risk
A-Churn. Personnel turnover	Completion bonuses; Pair programming
A-Skill. Not enough people skilled in agile methods	Hire customer programmer
Risks of using plan-driven methods	
P-Change. Rapid change	Short iterations; Simple design
P-Speed. Need for rapid results	Short iterations; Pair programming; Timeboxing
P-Emerge. Emergent requirements	Short iterations; Dedicated customer
P-Skill. Not enough people skilled in plan-driven methods	Low-Risk

Very Large Application: National Information System for Crisis Management (NISCM)

Under the leadership of the National Survivability Office (NSO), a broad coalition of government agencies and critical private-sector organizations is being formed to provide more rapid identification, prevention,

Broad coalition of government and private sector

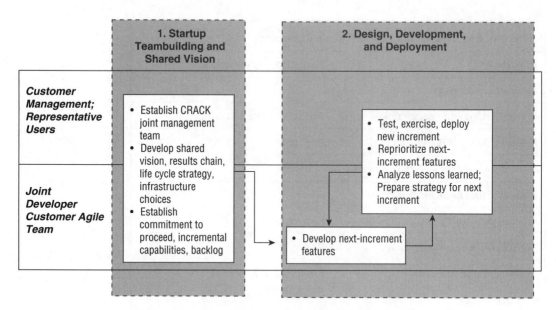

Figure 5-7   Overall Event Managers Project Strategy

assessment, management, and resolution of potential national crises. These crises include natural disasters; financial, biomedical, and weapons-oriented crises; and crises involving the national infrastructure: transportation, communication, information processing, and distribution of electricity, energy, and other critical resources and supplies.

Agent-based coordination of crisis activities

A major component of the initiative is a National Information System for Crisis Management. The NISCM will use the best of modern information technology to support cross-agency and public-private sector coordination of crisis management activities. Besides modern adaptive mobile network technology, virtual collaboration technology, information assurance technology, and information integration technology, the use of agent-based planning and monitoring technology is a major NISCM solution component.

The variety of crisis domains and key technologies makes it infeasible to contract with a single company to develop the full NISCM. The NSO has organized the NISCM acquisition around the use of a private-sector system-of-systems integration contractor. This integration contractor would develop and evolve the integrating information architecture for the NISCM; would subcontract development and evolution of the NISCM component systems; and would integrate, test, deploy, and coordinate support of incremental NISCM releases.

Integration contractor with many subcontractors

After two rounds of competitive concept definition, prototyping, architecture analysis, organizational teambuilding, and management planning, the NSO has selected Information Integrators Inc. (I3) to be the NISCM integrating contractor. An ambitious schedule has been established for the NISCM, including relatively easy-to-achieve early milestones involving integration of existing capabilities, and leading to a fully capable, fully operational version of the NISCM by the end of the decade.

I3 selected as integrator

Step 1: NISCM Project Risk Ratings

Since the NISCM will be a huge network including many independently evolving systems with different owners and objectives, and since millions of lives may be affected by its operation, a great deal of discipline will be involved in getting it to work effectively. However, since its objectives, threat profiles, components, and technologies will be rapidly changing, it will need a great deal of agility as well. In comparison to the intermediate-sized supply chain application, NISCM has dramatically challenging environmental risks, agile risks, and plan-driven risks.

Large, critical system with rapidly changing environment and requirements

NISCM Environmental Risks

In the environmental risk area, technology risks (*E-Tech*) include national-level scalability of adaptive mobile networks, virtual collaboration

High technical risks

technologies, information assurance technologies, and agent coordination technologies—plus compound risks involving their operational interactions. Multistakeholder coordination (*E-Coord*) is another, much larger source of risks, including technology-domain risks of coordinating many independently evolving development and operational processes, and political-domain risks involving information-is-power organizational turf and control issues.

Acquisition strategy adds coordination and complexity risk

A new set of major environmental risks involves the large number of information technology subcontractors to be evaluated, selected, integrated, and continuously coordinated into a collaborative team of normally competitive information technology contractors. An example challenge is that they all will have independently evolving choices of infrastructure capabilities, COTS products, and support tools (*E-Cmplx*).

Risk of inadequate COTS management

COTS product coordination is another source of risk. NISCM will have hundreds of independently evolving COTS products among its subcontracted components and affiliated systems. Many of them were not designed to interoperate. Surveys indicate that COTS products undergo new releases every eight to nine months and become unsupported after about three releases.[12] Just keeping track of their release status will be difficult, and ensuring interoperability and vendor support even more difficult.

Schedule is aggressive

Another significant general risk is the ambitious seven-year schedule. Comparison with other major national software systems indicates that NISCM would have considerably more than 10 million lines of code to develop. Most current software estimation models indicate that a single 10-million-line block of code will take at least nine years to develop.

NISCM Agile Risks

At the system-of-systems level, the scalability risks of using many of the agile technologies become prohibitive. The cost of late system-of-systems changes will be much higher than of early changes (*A-Scale*), making simple design and YAGNI infeasible (*A-YAGNI*). This is particularly true for critical system-of-systems-wide level-of-service objectives such as information security, graceful degradation, and sensor-decision-maker-effector performance timelines, which cannot be addressed by belated system-of-systems refactoring or by adding simple Band-Aids to each subcontractor's information architecture.

Size means scalability and YAGNI risks

The scale, diversity, and normal personnel turnover involved in the plethora of agencies, private-sector operators, and subcontractors makes a heavy dependence on tacit knowledge infeasible (*A-Churn*). It also makes it infeasible to issue monthly NISCM-wide releases in the expectation of smooth operational transitions. A considerably longer release interval will be needed to coordinate retraining and associated business process reengineering across multiorganization operational interfaces. However, pilot beta testing of monthly releases would be feasible and valuable.

Churn reduces effectiveness of tacit knowledge

NISCM Plan-Driven Risks

Although more plan-driven methods will be needed for much of NISCM, the rapidly evolving NISCM objectives, threats, organizations, components, and technologies make the use of a fixed, heavyweight set of plans and specifications highly risky. Their changes would be very difficult to coordinate across the wide collection of stakeholders (*P-Change*). A similar risk applies to the fact that many of the requirements will be emerging through use rather than being determinable in advance (*P-Emerge*).

Change and emergence complicate planning

Ambitious schedule adds development speed risks

The ambitious schedule creates both a need for plan-driven architectural specifications and a risk of overly detailed plans and specifications. On one hand, the lack of well-validated interface specifications for the many subcontractors will cause significant delay and rework to fix once their incompatibilities and infeasibilities are found downstream. On the other hand, if the plans and specifications are made too detailed and hard to change, the dynamism of the NISCM requirements, technology, and environment will cause excessive delay in reworking the plans and specifications (*P-Speed*). Here again, the concept of risk-based levels of detail can help find the most appropriate levels of detail.

Step 2: Compare the Agile and Plan-Driven Risks

Agile risks abound

Table 5-7 shows the NISCM risk profile compared to the previous projects. Figure 5-8 is the home ground polar graph. The risk ranges for agile methods indicate that there are parts of NISCM (e.g., GUI displays for the decision support systems) that are highly attractive and low-risk areas for using agile methods. But there are other parts of NISCM (e.g., coordinating multicontractor tiers to develop a large-scale, safety-critical, secure system) that are very high risk for agile methods.

But so do plan-driven risks

Likewise, there are also significant risks in using highly plan-driven approaches to NISCM. Thus, the project needs to go through Step 3 of the process. The next question is, "How much planning is enough to get Steps 3 and 4 right before proceeding into development?" The answer can be visualized by comparing the risk profiles for NISCM and the medium-sized SupplyChain.com project.

Planning Risk Exposure Profile

Sweet spot moves far right—considerable planning needed

As shown in Figure 5-9, the resulting risk exposure profile for the very large NISCM application moves the "How much planning is enough?" sweet spot considerably to the right toward more plans and considerably

Table 5-7 Risk Ratings for Three Example Systems

Risk Items	Risk Ratings		
	Event Managers	**Supply Chain.com**	**NISCM**
Environmental risks			
E-Tech. Technology uncertainties	■	■■	■■■
E-Coord. Many stakeholders	□	■	■■■
E-Cmplx. Complex system of systems	□	■	■■■
Risks of using agile methods			
A-Scale. Scalability and criticality	□	■■	■■–■■■■
A-YAGNI. Use of simple design	□	■■	■■–■■■■
A-Churn. Personnel turnover	■■	■	■■
A-Skill. Not enough people skilled in agile methods	□	■	■■–■■■
Risks of using plan-driven methods			
P-Change. Rapid change	■■■■	■■	■■
P-Speed. Need for rapid results	■■■■	■■	■■
P-Emerge. Emergent requirements	■■■■	■■	■■
P-Skill. Not enough people skilled in plan-driven methods	□	■	■■

Risk rating scale:
□—Minimal risk
■—Moderate risk
■■—Serious but manageable risk
■■■—Very serious but manageable risk
■■■■—Showstopper risk

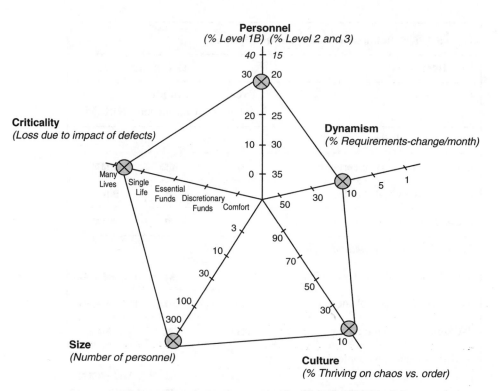

Figure 5-8   Home Ground Polar Chart for NISCM

upwards toward higher levels of risk than the intermediate-sized supply chain application.

Schedule and tiers of contractors drive need for architecture

The risk exposure due to rework delays goes up significantly. The probability of loss for inadequate planning and architecting goes up through creating more sources of rework. The size of loss for inadequate architecting goes up significantly because the fixes are more costly and because inadequate fixes have more safety consequences. The risk exposure due to planning delays goes up somewhat because of the increased size of loss of reworking detailed plans and specifications to accommodate change, but the increase is considerably less than that due to rework delays.

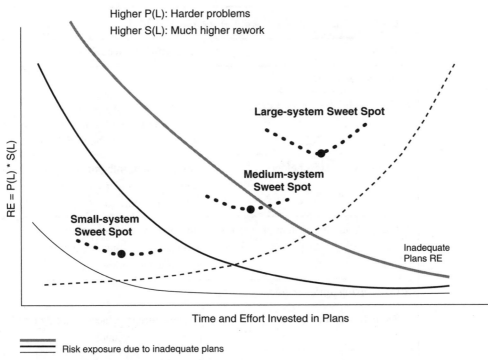

Figure 5-9 labels within the figure:

Higher P(L): Harder problems
Higher S(L): Much higher rework

Large-system Sweet Spot

Medium-system Sweet Spot

Small-system Sweet Spot

Inadequate Plans RE

RE = P(L) * S(L)

Time and Effort Invested in Plans

Risk exposure due to inadequate plans

Risk exposure due to market share erosion

Sum of risk exposures

**Figure 5-9   Risk Exposure Profile:
Very Large Crisis Management Application**

Steps 3 and 4: Risk-Based Strategy for NISCM System Development

The NISCM Program Manager for NSO and the NISCM Project Manager for I3 convened an Integrated Product Team of CRACK stakeholder representatives and discipline specialists to assess the general, agile, and plan-driven NISCM risks, and to lay out a risk-based process framework used to balance agility and discipline for the NISCM project. The results are shown in Table 5-8 and Figure 5-10.

CRACK stakeholder team develops plans

Table 5-8 NISCM Risk Mitigation Strategies	
Risk Items	**Mitigation Approaches**
Environmental risks	
E-Tech. Technology uncertainties	Major technology performance and scalability prototypes and early builds; Technology and COTS watch
E-Coord. Many stakeholders	Results chain; Integrated product teams; Stakeholder win-win; Award fee for collaboration
E-Cmplx. Complex system of systems	Complexity assessment and avoidance; Architecture determination and evaluation
Risks of using agile methods	
A-Scale. Scalability and criticality	Architecture interfaces enabling rapid parallel development
A-YAGNI. Use of simple design	Use within agile module teams; Use risk-based specification level of detail
A-Churn. Personnel turnover	Project completion bonuses; Personnel backups; Peer reviews and/or pair programming
A-Skill. Not enough people skilled in agile methods	Key personnel selection criteria; Project completion bonus
Risks of using plan-driven methods	
P-Change. Rapid change	Change-prescient architecture; Encapsulated agile method module teams; Agility award fee criterion
P-Speed. Need for rapid results	Schedule as independent variable; Architecture interfaces enabling rapid parallel development

Risk Items	Mitigation Approaches
Risks of using plan-driven methods	
P-Emerge. Emergent requirements	Evolutionary spiral development; Agile module teams
P-Skill. Not enough people skilled in plan-driven methods	Key personnel selection criteria; Project completion bonuses

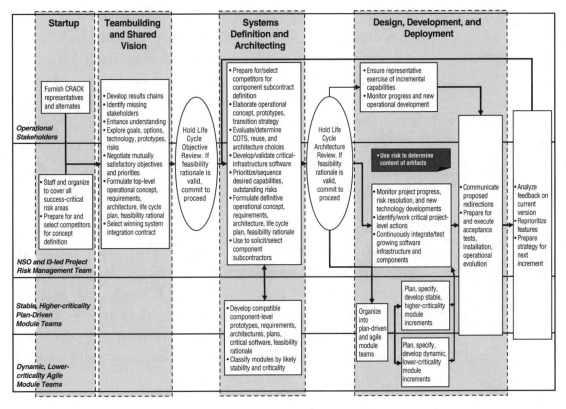

Figure 5-10   Overall NISCM Project Strategy

The SupplyChain.com strategy framework is viable, but needs extension

Compared to the process framework for the supply chain application in Figure 5-4, the NISCM process framework needs several extensions to cover the larger number of stakeholders, components, and risks involved in the very large NISCM application. But the basic process framework remains viable, as we are finding in similar, very large system-of-systems projects such as the U.S. Army Future Combat Systems project.

Mitigations for environmental risks are varied

✗ See Appendix D2

The NISCM *E-Tech* risks involving technology performance, scalability, and maturity risks are addressed by extensive prototyping, modeling, simulation, analysis, early development of high-risk modules, and continuing technology and COTS watch activities. The many-stakeholders *E-Coord* risks are addressed via results chains and integrated product teams bringing stakeholders together to ensure results chain feasibility and execution. Stakeholder collaboration is facilitated via win-win negotiations and contract award fees that reward collaboration efforts. The *E-Cmplx* complexity risks are addressed by feature prioritization using both mission importance and development complexity as criteria, and the development and review of a system architecture feasibility rationale.

Agile risks call for architecture and contract management activities

Risks of agile method scalability (*A-Scale*) and use of simple design (*A-YAGNI*) are addressed by developing relatively stable and change-prescient architecture interfaces within which multiple agile and plan-driven teams can build and evolve software in parallel with minimum ripple effects. Personnel skills and turnover risk (*A-Skill, P-Skill,* and *A-Churn*) are dealt with by key personnel selection criteria in source selection, project completion bonuses for performers, and knowledge sharing via mentoring, peer reviews, or pair programming.

Risks of excessive breakage in plans and specifications due to rapid change (*P-Change*) or emergent requirements (*P-Emerge*) are addressed by change-prescient architectures (identifying foreseeable sources of change and encapsulating them within modules), encapsulated agile module teams addressing the least-foreseeable sources of change (e.g., user interfaces, threat countermeasures), and contract award fee criteria rewarding adaptability to change as well as building to specifications. Risks of need for rapid results (*P-Speed*) are addressed by evolutionary spiral development, and the Schedule As Independent Variable (SAIV) approach (a scalable version of timeboxing).

Plan-driven risks call for team organization, architecture, and collaboration approaches

 See Appendix D3

The major stakeholder classes shown for NISCM in Figure 5-10 are similar to those in Figure 5-4. NISCM has a larger number of operational stakeholders—the key government and private-sector organizations involved. There is a larger Project and Risk Management team, consisting of the NSO project office, the I3 integration contractor, plus additional external specialists needed to cover the major risk areas (e.g., scalable adaptive mobile networks, information assurance, or scalable agent coordination).

Larger Project and Risk Management team

The other new stakeholders are the large number of subcontractors and sub-subcontractors to be chosen as best-of-breed solution providers in special solution areas. These areas would likely include sensor data processing, domain-specific data fusion and decision support, virtual collaboration support, adaptive mobile networks, geolocation services, specialized agent-based systems, logistics management, or special crisis management solution capabilities in the finance, biomedical, energy, defense, or urban services sectors.

Subcontractors are new stakeholders

The subcontractors will need to have well-defined statements of work and interface specifications to ensure effective interoperation of the NISCM components, but they will also need enough flexibility to adapt

Statements of work are critical for the subcontractors

to the various sources of NISCM change. This presents three primary risk-based solution elements to be addressed by the program and project managers and the NISCM Risk Management team:

1. How much detail is enough to provide in subcontractor specifications?
2. How to establish balances of agility and discipline for a wide variety of subcontractors?
3. How much time and effort is enough to invest in developing functional, performance, and interface specifications for the subcontractors?

Let's look at applying risk-based solutions to these "How much is enough?" questions.

Level of Detail of Subcontractor Specification

Risk-based specifications balance rigor and flexibility

The concept of risk-based specifications[13] provides a way to balance rigor and flexibility in subcontractor specifications. If it is a high risk *not* to specify rigorously and a low risk to do so, then specify it rigorously (e.g., performance-critical or dependability-critical multisubcontractor interfaces). If it is a low risk *not* to specify rigorously and a high risk to do so, then don't specify it rigorously (e.g., graphic user interfaces for long-range planning).

Subcontractors' Balance of Agility and Discipline

Motivation for subcontractors to remain as agile as possible

First, the subcontractors need a motivation to participate in NISCM team efforts to respond to change rather than to build software to prespecified requirements. This means that the subcontract solicitations should:

- Identify the portions of the NISCM architecture most likely to change, and indicate how they are likely to change.

- Request bidders to identify parametric interfaces for such change areas (e.g., for the number and types of data inputs to a decision analysis function).

- Establish award fee criteria for successful team performance in adaptation to changes.

Second, I3 needs to establish a process for determining which parts of the subcontractors' software should be developed using agile methods and which parts developed by plan-driven methods. From the agile and plan-driven home ground characteristics, I3 identifies relative criticality and relative requirements stability as the discriminators for selecting the methods used to develop each part of each subcontractor's software.

I3 must assign agile/plan-driven components for subcontractors

Thus, as shown in Figure 5-10, bidders would initially be asked to propose software development plans and an architecture organized around high-criticality, high-stability modules proposed for plan-driven development teams, and low-criticality, low-stability modules to be developed by agile development teams. Winning subcontractors (those with the most convincing plans and architectures) would then organize into plan-driven and agile teams, and develop the software to those plans. Of course the plans would need to adapt to unforeseen changes.

Bids include development plans and architectural concepts

Amount of Time Invested in Developing Subcontract Specifications

I3 could use some rule of thumb or comparison to similar projects to determine the amount of time to spend in risk mitigation and architecting the system. However, there are ways to quantitatively apply calibrated models to the problem. Figure 5-11 represents such an analysis using the COCOMO II tool. Details on the technique used and other technical material can be found in Appendix E2.

Architecture investment is key

See Appendix E2

Use COCOMO II factor to determine how much architecting is enough

In a nutshell, the analysis uses the *Architecture and Risk Resolution* (RESL) factor to determine rework costs for a range of software size estimates and indicates that as the amount of project schedule devoted to architecting and risk resolution decreases from over 40 percent down to 5 percent, the extra rework effort increases exponentially with the size of the software. Here are some examples:

- For a 10,000 KSLOC project such as NISCM, the sweet spot is about 40 percent. If you only invest 5 percent in architecting you will nearly double development time.
- For a 10 KSLOC project such as Event Managers, the sweet spot is at 5 percent. More than 5 percent architecting investment unnecessarily increases schedule.

Don't overinterpret the graph

We definitely need to inject a note of caution on overinterpretation of this simple model. It abstracts away such factors as the operational criticality of the application, which will move the sweet spot to the right, or the volatility of the requirements, which will move the sweet spot to the left. As a general caveat to using models, it is good to remember that old adage, "All models are wrong. Some are more useful than others."

Summary

Risk analysis can help establish and maintain balance

As shown above, risk analysis can help answer a variety of "How much is enough?" questions by balancing the risks of doing too little of something with the risk of doing too much. Besides showing qualitative analyses addressing risks for the small, medium, and very large agent-based planning applications, Figure 5-11 shows how these analyses can be quantified by using the COCOMO II Architecture and Risk Resolution scale factor. Similar analyses could be done with other software

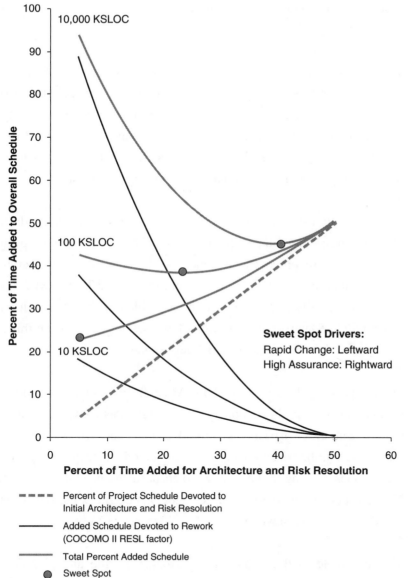

Figure 5-11   How Much Architecting Is Enough?

cost estimation models, but with less visibility into their proprietary cost estimating relationships.

Compare the risk patterns for the three systems

Table 5-9 (a repeat of Table 5-7) summarizes the results of applying Step 1 of the process (rating each project's general, agile, and plan-driven risks) to each of the example projects. For the small event planning application, the plan-driven risks clearly dominate the agile-oriented risks, with several very serious plan-driven risks. Step 2b thus leads the event planning application to adopt a home ground agile approach.

SupplyChain.com is a hybrid

For the medium-sized supply chain application, neither the agile nor plan-driven risks dominate, leading the supply chain project to develop a risk-based agile process with some plan-driven elements. Remember, however, that in some environments, an experienced TSP or RUP team could successfully implement a risk-based plan-driven approach with some agile elements, and that only a few changes could make this the more desirable way to approach the development.

NISCM is also a hybrid, but with higher risks and more planning and architecting

Some aspects of the very large NISCM application—its size and complexity—are clearly showstoppers for pure agile methods such as simple design. But other aspects—the rapid change and emergent requirements—are higher risks for plan-driven methods than for agile. Step 3 then applies, leading to the strategy to encapsulate the agile parts of the NISCM application, to go risk-based agile in the agile parts, and go risk-based plan-driven elsewhere.

The method can guide balancing the project development strategy

This tailorable method enables us to balance agile and plan-driven methods in a project development strategy. It can help organizations and projects take advantage of the benefits of both agile and plan-driven methods, while mitigating many of their drawbacks. Versions of the process are currently being used on several small projects, as well as for

Table 5-9 Risk Ratings for Three Example Systems			
Risk Items	**Risk Ratings**		
	Event Managers	**Supply Chain.com**	**NISCM**
Environmental risks			
E-Tech. Technology uncertainties	■	■■	■■■
E-Coord. Many stakeholders	□	■	■■■
E-Cmplx. Complex system of systems	□	■	■■■
Risks of using agile methods			
A-Scale. Scalability and criticality	□	■■	■■–■■■■
A-YAGNI. Use of simple design	□	■■	■■–■■■■
A-Churn. Personnel turnover	■■	■	■■
A-Skill. Not enough people skilled in agile methods	□	■	■■–■■■
Risks of using plan-driven methods			
P-Change. Rapid change	■■■	■■	■■
P-Speed. Need for rapid results	■■■	■■	■■
P-Emerge. Emergent requirements	■■■	■■	■■
P-Skill. Not enough people skilled in plan-driven methods	□	■	■■

Risk rating scale:
□—Minimal risk
■—Moderate risk
■■—Serious but manageable risk
■■■—Very serious but manageable risk
■■■■—Showstopper risk

the planning and risk management on a very large project. A related approach called Code Science or AgilePlus has been used successfully on over a dozen projects up to 400 KSLOC in size. It uses most of the XP practices plus a componentized architecture, risk-based situation audits, business analyses, and on-demand automatic document generation.[14, 15]

6

Conclusions

After you find the gold, there's still the job of picking out your particular nuggets.

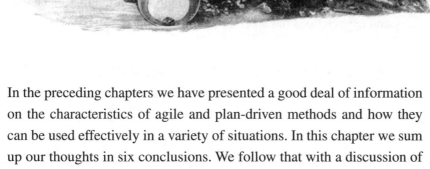

In the preceding chapters we have presented a good deal of information on the characteristics of agile and plan-driven methods and how they can be used effectively in a variety of situations. In this chapter we sum up our thoughts in six conclusions. We follow that with a discussion of how your organization can assess your current agility-discipline balance and then improve it to better fit your organization's evolving goals.

Conclusions focus on most frequent situations

Be forewarned that we will make some pretty heroic generalizations across wide swaths of agile and plan-driven methods. While we feel that each agile and plan-driven method shares some aspect of our assessment approach, we are aware that there is considerable variability in degree of applicability.

NB: Generalizations ahead

The Top Six Conclusions

Our top six conclusions are

1. Neither agile nor plan-driven methods provide a silver bullet.
2. Agile and plan-driven methods have home grounds where one clearly dominates the other.
3. Future trends are toward application developments that need both agility and discipline.
4. Some balanced methods are emerging.
5. It is better to build your method up than to tailor it down.
6. Methods are important, but potential silver bullets are more likely to be found in areas dealing with people, values, communication, and expectations management.

No Agile or Plan-Driven Method Silver Bullet

Essential difficulties are complexity, conformity, changeability, and invisibility

Neither agile nor plan-driven methods provide a methodological silver bullet that slays Fred Brooks' software engineering werewolf.[1] The nature of the werewolf concerns what Brooks calls the essential software engineering difficulties of coping with software's complexity, conformity, changeability, and invisibility. Some techniques have achieved the level of "lead bullets" in that they can slay normal wolves—that is, they can adequately solve some part of the software engineering problem. Elements of both agile and plan-driven approaches may be characterized as lead bullets.

Agile methods founder on complexity and conformity

Agile methods handle changeability and invisibility by building a shared vision of the project's objectives and strategies into each team member's shared store of tacit knowledge. But agile methods founder on handling complexity and to some extent conformity. They do not scale up to large complex projects, nor do they address conformity to such often-critical constraints as interface specifications or product line architectures. The ThoughtWorks lease management project discussed in Chapter 4 is a good example of how elements of plan-driven methods must be added to scale the agile project up to 50 people.

Plan-driven methods handle conformity and invisibility by investing in extensive documentation. Unfortunately, they founder on changeability (documentation rework) and the increasing complexity represented by systems-of-systems and enterprise integration.

Plan-driven methods founder on changeability and complexity

We have found that over the years, the increasingly rapid pace of change has identified a fallacy in the following assumption: If a software technique lead bullet can slay a software wolf this year, it will be able to slay the wolf's evolving offspring next year. Examples of techniques where this fallacy is apparent include

"Lead bullets" founder on changeability

- The sequential, requirements-first waterfall process model that could work quite well for 1960s or 1970s batch, sequential, noninteractive applications.
- Pre-WYSIWYG* word processing systems organized around separate edit, format, and runoff modules.
- Pre-Web book sales management systems that could not keep up with amazon.com.

Other examples of lead-bullet techniques with dwindling (but still important) niches are fixed-contract software management models, heavyweight formal methods, and static domain and enterprise architectures.

Some lead bullets are losing potency

*WYSIWYG: What You See Is What You Get.

*Polar chart identifies
dimensions of agile
and plan-driven
home grounds*

Agile and Plan-Driven Method Home Grounds

There are definite home grounds for pure agile and pure plan-driven methods, although there are very few methods at the extremes. There is a relationship with a method's position between the home grounds and the type of project and environment where it will most likely succeed. The five critical factors described in Chapter 2 and illustrated in the home ground polar chart (Figure 6-1) can help establish where a particular project or organization may be with respect to those home grounds.

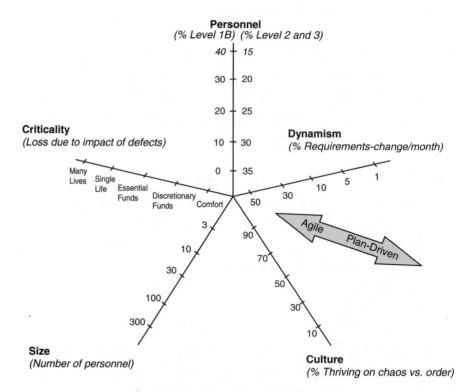

Figure 6-1   Home Ground Polar Chart

Future Applications Will Need Both Agility and Discipline

In the past, there have been many small, noncritical, well-skilled, agile-culture, rapidly evolving projects occupying the agile home ground in the center of Figure 6-1. There have also been many people working on large, critical, mixed-skill, ordered-culture, stable projects occupying the plan-driven home ground at the periphery of the chart. However, things are changing.

Both agility and discipline are critical to future software success

Large projects can no longer count on low rates of change, and their extensive process and product plans will become expensive sources of rework and delay. As the use of agile methods progresses from individual early-adopter projects to enterprise-coupled mainstream applications, the Brooksian software development werewolves of complexity and conformity will be waiting for them. Thus, there will be a higher premium on having methods available that combine agility and discipline in situation-tailorable ways.

Maintaining plans will become increasingly expensive, but complexity and conformity must be addressed

Balanced Agility-Discipline Methods Are Emerging

The projects discussed in Chapter 4 are individual examples of balancing agile and plan-driven methods that provide pointers on how to achieve balance. Some of the agile methods, such as Crystal Orange, DSDM, FDD, and Lean Development, have emerging approaches for achieving balance. The same is true of new, lighter versions of the Rational Unified Process.

There are successful examples and maturing methods for achieving balance

The tailorable method defined in Chapter 5 provides a risk-driven, spiral-type approach for balancing agile and plan-driven methods. It is not fully developed, but has worked well in situations where it has been applied. It is definitely not a cookbook approach; each project will need some thought to apply it to the particular situation.

Chapter 5 offers some guidance

Build Your Method Up—Don't Tailor It Down

Start small and add rigor as needed

As we have discussed under Management Characteristics in Chapter 2, plan-driven methods have had a tradition of developing all-inclusive methods that can be tailored down to fit a particular situation. Experts can do this, but nonexperts tend to play it safe and use the whole thing, often at considerable unnecessary expense. Agilists offer a better approach of starting with relatively minimal sets of practices and only adding extras where they can be clearly justified by cost-benefit. In some cases, as with Crystal, they will have multiple core sets for different levels of size or criticality. As we have seen with RUP, efforts are under way to develop similar approaches for building up plan-driven methods.

Focus Less on Methods—More on People, Values, Communication, and Expectations Management

Good people and teams trump other factors

The agilists have it right in valuing individuals and interactions over process and tools. They are not the first to emphasize this. There is a long list of wake-up calls—Weinberg's 1971 *Psychology of Computer Programming*,[2] the Scandinavian participatory design movement,[3] DeMarco and Lister's 1987 *Peopleware*,[4] and Curtis's studies of people factors[5] and development of the People Capability Maturity Model.[6] There is also a wealth of corroborative evidence that people factors dominate other software cost and quality drivers, such as the 1986 Grant-Sackman experiments showing 26:1 variations in people's performance[7] and the 1981 and 2000 COCOMO and COCOMO II cost model calibrations showing 10:1 effects of personnel capability, experience, and continuity.[8, 9] But the agilists may finally provide a critical mass of voices amplifying this message.

People

Software engineering is done "of the people, by the people and for the people."

Software engineering is of, by, and for the people

- *Of the People.* People organize themselves into teams to develop mutually satisfactory software systems.
- *By the People.* People identify what software capabilities they need, and other people develop it for them.
- *For the People.* People pay the bills for software development and use the resulting products.

Unfortunately, software engineering is still struggling with a "separation of concerns" legacy that contends translating requirements into code is so hard that it must be accomplished in isolation from people concerns. A few quotes will illustrate the situation:

Legacy of requirements separated from people

> The notion of "user" cannot be precisely defined, and therefore it has no place in computer science or software engineering.[10]

> Analysis and allocation of the system requirements is not the responsibility of the software engineering group, but it is a prerequisite for their work.[11]

> Software engineering is not project management.[12]

In today's and tomorrow's world, where software decisions increasingly drive system outcomes, this separation of concerns is increasingly harmful. Good agilist treatments of people and their ecosystems are provided in Jim Highsmith's *Agile Software Development Ecosystems*[13] and Alistair Cockburn's *Agile Software Development.*[14] Complementary plan-driven approaches are provided in Watts Humphrey's *Managing Technical People*[15] and his Personal Software Process,[16, 17] as well as the People Capability Maturity Model developed by Bill Curtis, Bill Hefley, and Sally Miller.[18]

Separation of concerns can be harmful

Values

Value-neutral methods can be harmful

Along with people come values—different values. One of the most significant and underemphasized challenges in software engineering is to reconcile different users', customers', developers', and other success-critical stakeholders' value propositions about a proposed software system into a mutually satisfactory win-win system definition and outcome. Unfortunately, software engineering is caught in a value-neutral time warp, where every requirement, use case, object, test case, and defect is considered to be equally important. Most process improvement initiatives and debates, including the silver bullet debate, are inwardly focused on improving software productivity rather than outwardly focused on delivering higher value per unit cost to stakeholders. Again, agile methods and their attention to prioritizing requirements and responding to changes in stakeholder value propositions are pushing us in more high-payoff directions. Other aspects of value-based software engineering practices and payoffs are described in *Value-Based Software Engineering.*[19]

Communication

There are many software project communication needs and options

Even with closely knit, in-house development organizations, the "I can't express exactly what I need, but *I'll know it when I see it*" (IKIWISI) syndrome limits people's ability to communicate an advance set of requirements for a software system. If software definition and development occurs across organizational boundaries, even more communication work is needed to define and evolve a shared system vision and development strategy. The increasingly rapid pace of change exacerbates the problem and raises the stakes of inadequate communication.

Cockburn's Agile Software Development *helps sort them out*

Except for the landmark people-oriented sources mentioned above and a few others, there are frustratingly few sources of guidance and insight on what kinds of communication work best in what situations. Cockburn's *Agile Software Development* is a particularly valuable recent source. It gets its priorities right by not discussing methods until the fourth chapter, and spending the first hundred or so pages discussing why we have problems communicating and what can be done about it. It nicely characterizes software development as a cooperative game of invention and communication, and provides numerous helpful communication concepts and techniques. Some examples are the three skill levels discussed in Chapter 2, human success and failure modes, information radiators and convection currents, and the effects of distance on communication effectiveness. It's well worth reading, whatever your location along the agility-discipline spectrum.

Expectations Management

Our bottom-line conclusion at the end of the "day in the life" profiles of PSP/TSP and XP in Chapter 3 coincides with one of the major findings in a recent root-cause analysis of troubled DoD software projects.[20] It is that the differences between successful and troubled software projects is most often the difference between good and bad expectations management.

Poor expectations management causes many software project failures

Most software people do not do well at expectations management. They have a strong desire to please and to avoid confrontation, and have little confidence in their ability to predict software project schedules and budgets. This makes them a pushover for aggressive customers and managers trying to get more software for less time and money.

Difficulty lies in desire-to-please and confidence in estimates

The most significant factor in the PSP/TSP and XP teams in Chapter 3 is that they had enough process mastery, preparation, and courage to be able to get their customers to agree to reducing functionality or increasing schedule in return for accommodating a new high-priority change. They were aware that setting up unrealistic expectations was not a win for the customers either, and they were able to convince the customers to

Discipline (process mastery, preparation, and courage) helps manage expectations

scale back their expectations. Both agile short iterations and plan-driven productivity calibration are keys to successfully managing software expectations.

What Can You Do Next about Balancing Agility and Discipline?

Start with a self-assessment

In our era of increasingly rapid change, the most risky thing you can do is to continue with business as usual without doing a self-assessment of where your organization is, where its success-critical stakeholders want it to go, and how it will cope with future trends. Key stakeholders to consult include your users, customers, developers, suppliers, and strategic partners. Key future trends to consider include

- The increased pace of change and need for agility
- The increased concern with software dependability and need for discipline
- Your ability to satisfy your stakeholders' evolving value propositions and to keep up with your toughest competitors
- The increasing gap between supply and demand for Cockburn Levels 2 and 3 people
- Your ability to cope with existing and emerging technical challenges such as COTS integration, evolving Internet and Web capabilities, distributed and mobile operations, agent coordination, and multimode virtual collaboration

A good context for performing such a self-assessment is provided in Jim Collins' recent book, *Good to Great*.[21] Although its primary focus is at the corporate level, its emphasis on balancing shared internal self-discipline and entrepreneurial agility can be applied at the software development organization level as well. Collins' characterization of

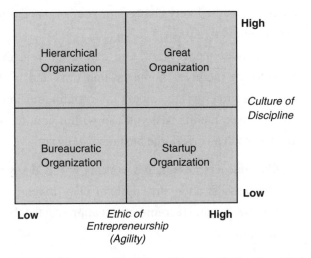

Figure 6-2   Collins' *Good-to-Great* **Matrix of Creative Discipline**

Adapted from *Good to Great: Why Some Companies Make the Leap . . . and Others Don't* by Jim Collins (HarperCollins). Copyright 2002 by Jim Collins. Used by permission.

how discipline and agility contribute to greatness is summarized in Figure 6-2.

If you have already done such an assessment, then you are ready to address the issue of how your organization should best balance agility and discipline. If not, you should at least take a first cut at a self-assessment so that you have some picture of where you are and where you want to go.

Steps toward Balancing Software Development Agility and Discipline

The steps below provide a simple recipe for balancing agility and discipline. Be sure, however, that you perform them in consultation with your key stakeholders.

A simple recipe for balancing agility and discipline

Step 1. Use Figure 6-1 to assess where your projects currently are with respect to the five key axes. If you have different organizations with different profiles, make separate assessments.

Use the five axes to map your home ground

Also, assess the likely changes in your organization's profile over the next five years.

A success strategy for an obvious home ground

Step 2. If your assessments show you comfortably in the agile or plan-driven methods' home ground now and in the future, your best strategy is to embark on a continuous improvement effort to become the best you can within your home ground. To start such an effort, the best next steps are

a. Convene a representative working group of key stakeholders to assess alternative agile or plan-driven improvement approaches and recommend an approach that best fits your situation.

b. Identify a reasonably tractable project, staffed with capable and enthusiastic people, to be trained in using the approach, to apply it, and to develop a plan for both dealing with problems encountered and for extending the approach across the organization.

c. Execute the plan for extending the approach, always including evaluation and feedback into continuous improvement during and after each project.

A success strategy for a home ground with anomalies

Step 3. If your Figure 6-1 assessments leave you mostly in the agile or plan-driven home grounds, but with some anomalies, treat the anomalies as risk factors to be added to the charters of the groups performing Steps 2a-c. Examples of potential anomalies are

a. Operating mostly in a plan-driven home ground, but in an increasingly dynamic marketplace.

b. Operating with agile fix-it-later developers with a growing, increasingly enterprise-integrated and dependability-oriented user base.

c. Finding that your technical people are successfully adapting to dynamism, but that your contract management people are not.

The first two anomalies can be addressed via the risk assessment and managerial techniques described in Chapter 5. The third would involve a more specialized approach to change management in the contracting organization, but done with their collaboration and the support of upper management.

If you have several organizations and several profiles, it is best to prioritize your approach to work on those you believe are most important and likely to achieve early successes. An exception is if there are projects in crisis that need, and are receptive to, significant help and redirection.

Focus initially on high-payoff early adopters

Step 4. If your Figure 6-1 assessments leave you with a highly mixed agile/plan-driven profile, you need to develop an incremental mixed strategy to take you from your current situation to the one you have chosen as a goal. For example, suppose that your organization primarily does 50-person, essential-funds critical projects with a mix of 20 percent Levels 2 and 3 and 30 percent Level 1B personnel, with dynamism rapidly increasing from 1 percent per month to 10 percent per month, a culture only 30 percent oriented toward thriving on chaos, and a corporate steady-state goal to do all software internally. This profile is shown in Figure 6-3.

A success strategy for a highly mixed organization

In this case, you would like to function internally like the teams doing the lease management example in Chapter 4 or the supply chain example in Chapter 5. If your staffing profile had 30 percent Levels 2 and 3 and 10 percent Level 1B people and your culture was 70 percent toward thriving on chaos, then you could apply the supply chain process and

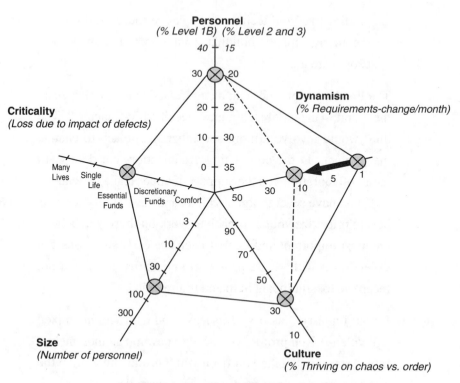

Figure 6-3   Sample Highly Mixed Profile

succeed internally. Unfortunately, your current staffing profile and culture make this infeasible.

*A strategic
partnership for
rapid change may
be attractive*

One option for you would be to start on a long-term internal effort to upgrade your staff and change your culture. But
a quicker and less risky approach would be to enter a strategic partnership with an agile methods company to serve as
near-term trainers, codevelopers, and mentors for your staff.
This would expedite an initiative to bring as many of your
Level 1A people up to Level 2 as possible, and to bring as
many of your Level 1B people up to Level 1A, at least in
some niche area. The agile methods company people could

also serve as change agents in making your organizational culture more thrive-on-chaos oriented.

In other cases, you might be a growing pure-agile company with a need to add more discipline and scalability to accommodate larger and more critical products. You could employ a similar strategy with a plan-driven services company to rapidly rebalance your operations, staff profile, and culture.

A similar strategy would apply for being more plan-driven

Step 5. Your organization should complement whatever agile/plan-driven balancing options it pursues with sustained effort to improve your staff capabilities, value-oriented capabilities, communication capabilities, and expectations management capabilities. It is also important to track your progress with respect to your plans and apply corrective action whenever new opportunities come up. A good checklist for staff capabilities is the People CMM. A good starting point for value-oriented capabilities is *Value-Based Software Engineering*.[22] A good mechanism for tracking multicriteria, multi-initiative programs is the Balanced Scorecard technique.[23] Naomi Karten's books are a good starting point for expectations management.[24, 25]

Improve your people, values, communication, and expectations management

Afterword

We hope we have provided you with the information and understanding needed to eliminate some of your perplexity regarding discipline and agility. The risk-based approach and analytic techniques presented are not "Yet Another Method," but represent a way to structure your thinking and take advantage of your personal insight in balancing discipline and agility within your own local environment.

We hope you are less perplexed

One cautionary note: The landscape of methods is geologically active and the geography is continuously changing. We encourage you to use some of the references in the appendices to stay in touch with both agile and plan-driven approaches as they adapt and evolve, and continuously question how that change could affect your organization and business goals. We believe that the risk-based framework described here will help you in that task.

Stay in touch— things change quickly in software

Appendix A

Comparing the Methods

In this appendix, we provide information about the various methods currently available and how they fit into this risk-based approach. We provide a thumbnail sketch of each method, graphically characterize it along three factor dimensions as shown in Table A-1,* and indicate any special considerations.

Profiles and thumbnail sketches for a variety of methods

Table A-1 Comparison Factor Table				
Levels of Concern	Business Enterprise	Business System	Multiteam Project	Single-Team Project	Individual
Life Cycle Activities	Concept Development	Requirements	Design	Development	Maintenance
Sources of Constraint	Management Processes	Technical Practices	Risk/ Opportunity	Measurement Practices	Customer Interface

*This characterization was inspired by material in *Agile Software Development Methods,* a VTT Electronics (Finland) report by Abrahamsson, Salo, Ronkainen, and Warsta.

Profile table covers key characteristics

In the profile table, an open circle (o) indicates partial applicability and a colored circle (●) means full applicability. The table characteristics are defined as:

1. **Levels of Concern.** This factor identifies the organizational scope for which the method provides specific guidance.
2. **Life Cycle Activities.** This factor identifies the life cycle activities for which the method provides specific guidance.
3. **Sources of Constraint.** Each method puts constraints on the implementor—the fewer the constraints, the more agile the method can be considered. We indicate the sources of constraint on five project areas: management processes, technical practices, risk/opportunity considerations, measurement practices, and the customer interface.

Middle-sized Chapter 6 project is rating base

Sometimes a method's degree of guidance depends on the level of size, criticality, or dynamism of the project. In order to be consistent about our ratings, we make them with respect to the middle-of-the-road project we provided method guidance for in Chapter 6.

Ranges are provided for risk- or opportunity-based methods

Another difficulty comes in rating strongly risk-driven or opportunity-driven methods such as ASD, CMMI, Crystal, DSDM, Lean Development, RUP, and TSP. These methods will use project risk patterns to push them toward more lightly constrained management practices for a small, noncritical, dynamic project, and more heavily constrained management processes for a large, critical, stable project. In such cases, we provide ranges for the degree of constraint imposed by the method.

Methods presented on a rough agility scale

Subject to this caveat, we have tried to approximately order the methods from most agile to most plan-driven, as defined by the scope and severity of the sources of constraint levied on the developer. Where the method is risk-based, a range of values is provided. There can certainly be disagreement with this ordering, but we believe it provides an approximate scale to help you survey the methods. Our order is shown in Table A-2. We have ranked the DSDM, RUP, and TSP, the three most comprehensive risk-driven methods, as equal in relation to sources of constraint and so list them in alphabetical order.

Table A-2 Methods Ordered by Number and Strength of Constraints						
Agility Rank	**Method**	**Very Low**	**Low**	**Med.**	**High**	**Very High**
1	Scrum	●				
2	Adaptive Software Development (ASD)	●	●	●		
3	Lean Development (LD)	●	●	●		
4	Crystal	●	●	●		
5	eXtreme Programming (XP)		●	●		
6	Dynamic Systems Development Method (DSDM)		●	●	●	
6	Rational Unified Process (RUP)		●	●	●	
6	Team Software Process (TSP)		●	●	●	
9	Feature-Driven Development (FDD)			●		
10	Capability Maturity Model Integration (CMMI)		●	●	●	●
11	Capability Maturity Model for Software (SW-CMM)				●	●
12	Personal Software Process (PSP)					●
13	Cleanroom					●

Scrum

Levels of Concern	Business Enterprise	Business System	Multiteam Project	Single-Team Project	Individual
		o	o	o	o
Life Cycle Activities	Concept Development	Requirements	Design	Development	Maintenance
	o	o	o	o	o
Sources of Constraint	Management Processes	Technical Practices	Risk/ Opportunity	Measurement Practices	Customer Interface
	●		o		o

Thumbnail Sketch

A project management approach

Scrum was developed by Ken Schwaber and Jeff Sutherland. Scrum is based on the concept that software development is not a defined process, but an empirical process with complex input/output transformations that may or may not be repeated under differing circumstances. The name is derived from a rugby play where the teams attempt to move against each other in large, brute-force groups. Each group must be quick to counter the other's thrusts and adjust to exploit any perceived weakness without the luxury of planning.

Project management emphasis based on a standard 30-day Sprint

Scrum has a definite project management emphasis. It is managed by a Scrum Master, who can be considered as much a consultant or coach as a manager. There is a fundamental 30-day development cycle (called a Sprint), which is preceded by pre-Sprint activities and post-Sprint activities. A short (less than 30 minutes) daily Scrum meeting allows the team to monitor status and communicate problems.

Project planning is based on a Product Backlog, which contains functions and technology enhancements envisioned for the project. Two meetings are held—one to decide the features for the next Sprint and the other to plan out the work. Additionally, a Sprint Goal is established, which serves as a minimum success criterion for the Sprint and acts to keep the team focused on the broader picture rather than narrowly on the task at hand.

Planning based on backlog

Comments

Scrum offers a means of introducing agile methods into a traditionally disciplined environment. By using Scrum for one or more components of the system, management can assess its effectiveness without completely changing the way the organization normally does business.

Amenable to traditional organizations

Scrum has been one of the few agile methods that has attempted to scale up for larger projects. This has been accomplished in much the same way as organizations handle integrated product teams. The individual Scrum team coaches are part of a higher echelon team of coaches that span several products. Maintaining communication and preventing conflicting development is handled through this coordinating team. Successful Scrum scaleups have involved a strong complement of Cockburn Level 3 personnel.

Scaled up to medium projects

References

Schwaber, K. 1995. "Scrum Development Process," OOPSLA'95. Workshop on Business Object Design and Implementation. Springer-Verlag.

Schwaber, K., and M. Beedle. 2002. *Agile Software Development with Scrum.* Upper Saddle River, NJ: Prentice-Hall.

www.controlchaos.com

Adaptive Software Development (ASD)

Levels of Concern	Business Enterprise	Business System	Multiteam Project	Single-Team Project	Individual
	o	o	o	o	
Life Cycle Activities	Concept Development	Requirements	Design	Development	Maintenance
	o	o	o	o	o
Sources of Constraint	Management Processes	Technical Practices	Risk/ Opportunity	Measurement Practices	Customer Interface
	o		●		o

Thumbnail Sketch

Continuous adaptation to the work at hand is normal

Adaptive Software Development grew out of rapid application development work by Jim Highsmith and Sam Bayer. ASD embodies the principle that continuous adaptation of the process to the work at hand is the normal state of affairs.

Based on a speculate- collaborate- learn cycle

ASD replaces the traditional waterfall cycle with a repeating series of *speculate, collaborate,* and *learn* cycles. This dynamic cycle provides for continuous learning and adaptation to the emergent state of the project. The characteristics of an ASD life cycle are that it is mission focused, feature based, iterative, timeboxed, risk driven, and change tolerant.

Comments

ASD is not "tidy"

ASD is designed to be managed "balanced on the edge of chaos." There aren't a lot of specifics on how things get done, just the outline of opportunities that the developing team must take advantage of. It would definitely take a Cockburn Level 3 guru to tailor ASD to a particular project situation.

ASD and its collaborative, nonprescriptive philosophy may be difficult to apply to large, critical, relatively stable development efforts.

May not scale to large, critical, stable projects

References

Highsmith, J.A. 2000. *Adaptive Software Development: A Collaborative Approach to Managing Complex Systems.* New York: Dorset House.
www.adaptivesd.com

Lean Development (LD)

Levels of Concern	Business Enterprise	Business System	Multiteam Project	Single-Team Project	Individual
	o	●	o		
Life Cycle Activities	Concept Development	Requirements	Design	Development	Maintenance
	o	o	o		o
Sources of Constraint	Management Processes	Technical Practices	Risk/ Opportunity	Measurement Practices	Customer Interface
	o–●		●		o

Thumbnail Sketch

The Lean Development methodology is a proprietary approach developed by Bob Charette. It evolved out of his expertise in risk management and the principles and vision of lean manufacturing concepts of Womack, Jones, and Roos. Charette sees agility as tolerance to change and has developed a three-tiered approach to competitiveness based on change. One key concept is "risk entrepreneurship," which he defines as the ability to turn risk into opportunity.

Based on risk management and lean manufacturing

More traditional complete life cycle framework

The LD process is made up of three phases: startup, steady state, and transition-renewal. While LD is product focused, it adds the dimension of domains or product lines, where software can be reused across several models of the same generic product. Overall planning is accomplished in the startup phase, where business cases and feasibility studies are completed. Steady state is a design-build phase made up of a series of short spirals. Once delivered, the product is maintained in a constant renewal and transition phase. Documentation is developed and delivered in this transition phase.

Focuses on the entire enterprise vs. specific software practices

While LD is team based, it is not limited to software development teams. It involves everyone in the product chain from the CEO down. LD is much more a business strategy and project management approach than a development process. LD is relatively nonspecific about particular software development practices, policies, and guidelines.

Comments

Strategic, risk-driven, enterprise-wide but proprietary

Highsmith has said that LD represents the first of the agile methods to address top executives. The strategic, risk/opportunity-based approach resonates with executives and management. At this point, LD is primarily a direct product of Charette's company ITABHI, which may make it more difficult to implement. LD embodies many of the characteristics of our risk-based approach to agility. Of the methods presented here, it has the most explicit focus on assessing and achieving business value.

References

Womack, J., D. Jones, D. Roos. 1991. *The Machine That Changed the World : The Story of Lean Production*. New York: HarperCollins.

Highsmith, J.A. 2002. *Agile Software Development Ecosystems*. Boston: Addison-Wesley.

www.itabhi.com

Crystal

Levels of Concern	Business Enterprise	Business System	Multiteam Project	Single-Team Project	Individual
		o	●	●	o
Life Cycle Activities	Concept Development	Requirements	Design	Development	Maintenance
	o	o	o	o	o
Sources of Constraint	Management Processes	Technical Practices	Risk/ Opportunity	Measurement Practices	Customer Interface
	o–●	o–●	●	o	o–●

Thumbnail Sketch

The Crystal family of methods was developed by Alistair Cockburn as an outgrowth of his global consulting efforts. Rather than a single method, Crystal provides a framework of related methods that address the variability of environment and specific characteristics of projects. The term "Crystal" is used as an extended metaphor to describe the "color" and "hardness" of each method.

Framework of multiple methods

There are numerous variations of the method that are selected according to the size of the development team and the criticality of the project undertaken. Each of the Crystal variations is named by color (Clear, Yellow, Orange, Red) to denote the number of people involved, and by "hardness" to denote the criticality in terms of the type of loss (Comfort, Discretionary money, Essential money, and Life) resulting from defects. Crystal methods share two values: They are people- and communication-centric, and they are highly tolerant. Currently, only two of the colors (Clear and Orange) have been fully elaborated.

Variation determined by size and criticality

*Strong where
well-defined, but
difficult elsewhere*

Comments

The risks of Crystal center on the ability of the practitioners to determine how to apply it outside the well-defined Crystal Clear and Orange elaborations. As opposed to ASD, however, a Crystal Clear or Crystal Orange project could be tailored by a Cockburn Level 2 person. Cockburn advocates the "lighter is better as long as it lasts" paradigm, which implies that there must be a significant consequence (or risk) before the team implements a harder version. Crystal addresses the need for project-specific methodologies and has many attributes that support our risk-based strategy.

References

Cockburn, A. 2002. *Agile Software Development.* Boston: Addison-Wesley.

Cockburn, A. 2000. *Writing Effective Use Cases: The Crystal Collection for Software Professionals.* Boston: Addison-Wesley.

http://alistair.cockburn.us

eXtreme Programming (XP)

Levels of Concern	Business Enterprise	Business System	Multiteam Project	Single-Team Project	Individual
		o		●	●
Life Cycle Activities	Concept Development	Requirements	Design	Development	Maintenance
		●	●	●	●
Sources of Constraint	Management Processes	Technical Practices	Risk/ Opportunity	Measurement Practices	Customer Interface
	o	●	o	o	●

Thumbnail Sketch

eXtreme Programming is the most widely recognized agile method. Kent Beck, Ward Cunningham, and Ron Jeffries based the method on their experiences at Daimler Chrysler and captured the attention of the world with its "in your face" name.

Widely recognized and used

XP is based on four values and an initial set of twelve practices, which have been extended in various ways since XP's introduction. The fundamental XP values are

Value based— four values

- **Communication.** Most projects fail because of poor communication, so implement practices that force communication in a positive fashion.
- **Simplicity.** Develop the simplest product that meets the customer's needs.
- **Feedback.** Developers must obtain and value feedback from the customer, from the system, and from each other.
- **Courage.** Be prepared to make hard decisions that support the other principles and practices.

Work is performed by small teams that include a *customer continuously present* on-site. XP begins with the *planning game,* where customers and developers negotiate requirements in the form of stories captured on index cards. The system concept is captured in terms of a *metaphor* to support a single vision of success. The fundamental *short cycle time* (iteration) is no more than three weeks. The technical process assumes *collective ownership* of the product so that anyone can work on anything. This fits with *simple design, pair programming,* and emergent design through *refactoring* to work. *Coding standards* are established by the team, and quality is assured through a *test-first approach* and

Twelve core practices

continuous integration. A sustainable pace is achieved through emphasis on a *40-hour work week.*

Comments

*Primary issue
is scaling*

XP has a strong track record for achieving success in small applications. Scaling is an issue, with a 20-person team often stated as an absolute upper limit. While discipline-enhanced versions of XP have been shown to work with multiple teams (see Chapter 4), there has been relatively little experience using it in that environment. Simple design and YAGNI are often inappropriate for stable systems with predictable evolution. Beck identifies several other barriers to using XP, including teams that are not collocated, long feedback cycles, and long integration processes. Chapter 3 provides an example of the use of XP.

Reference

Beck, K. 1999. *Extreme Programming Explained: Embracing Change.* Reading, MA: Addison-Wesley.

Dynamic Systems Development Method (DSDM)

Levels of Concern	Business Enterprise	Business System	Multiteam Project	Single-Team Project	Individual
	o	●	●	●	o
Life Cycle Activities	Concept Development	Requirements	Design	Development	Maintenance
	●	●	o	o	o
Sources of Constraint	Management Processes	Technical Practices	Risk/ Opportunity	Measurement Practices	Customer Interface
	●	o	●	o	o

Thumbnail Sketch

DSDM is an independent development approach that is more a framework for developing the software than a particular method. Emerging in 1994, it was developed by and continues to evolve under the auspices of the DSDM Consortium. The Consortium was established to develop and promote a public domain rapid application development method. It has a significant support infrastructure in place, including multiple books, courses, and user groups throughout the world, although the majority of users are in Europe and Great Britain.

Large framework with majority of users in Europe and Great Britain

There are five phases in the DSDM process: Feasibility, Business Study, Functional Model Iteration, Design and Build Iteration, and Implementation. The Feasibility and Business Study phases are performed sequentially, with their results informing the remaining iterative and incremental phases. Once the product has been implemented in the target environment, the project goes into a maintenance posture until new feasibility and business studies can be completed.

Five-phase process

The DSDM life cycle provides strong emphasis for project management activities. Planning is inherent in each phase, as plans evolve based on the increments and their results. Detailed contents for plans are defined. Timeboxing is the primary means of planning, monitoring, and controlling. Schedule and cost generally are held constant, with the requirements to be implemented as the dependent variable. Requirements are prioritized using the MoSCoW (Must have, Should have, Could have, Want) technique. Scripts that define management activities throughout the life cycle are provided by the method. Work products are defined and described for each DSDM phase. A risk management process based on stated principles is provided.

Strong process management emphasis

Scalable teams with 10 defined roles

DSDM is designed for small teams, but can be scaled to almost any size. There are 10 project roles defined in DSDM, each with specific skills, responsibilities, and activities. These roles are not necessarily independent individuals, but may be shared or combined as fits the project.

Comments

"Heavy" agile may minimize agile benefits

DSDM has many similarities to RUP and TSP. As with RUP and TSP, it has a significant amount of structure and counts on its use of risk management to achieve greater agility than with traditional disciplined processes. It has a more explicit emphasis on a minimalist interpretation of its guidance than RUP or TSP.

Strong infrastructure and more traditional feel

The key advantage to DSDM is the infrastructure and level of documentation available to implement it. The method feels more like traditional development processes and so may be easier to adopt for process-based organizations.

References

DSDM Consortium. 1997. *Dynamic Systems Development Method, Version 3.* Ashford, England: DSDM Consortium.

Stapleton, J. 2003. *DSDM: Business Focused Development (2nd Ed.).* Boston: Addison-Wesley.

Stapleton, J. 1997. *DSDM, Dynamic Systems Development Method: The Method in Practice.* Reading, MA: Addison-Wesley.

www.dsdm.org

Rational Unified Process (RUP)

Levels of Concern	Business Enterprise	Business System	Multiteam Project	Single-Team Project	Individual
		o	●	●	
Life Cycle Activities	Concept Development	Requirements	Design	Development	Maintenance
	●	●	●	●	●
Sources of Constraint	Management Processes	Technical Practices	Risk/ Opportunity	Measurement Practices	Customer Interface
	o	o	●	o	

Thumbnail Sketch

The Rational Unified Process was developed concurrently with the Unified Modeling Language (UML) derived by Rational Corporation (now a division of IBM) from several object-oriented analysis and design methods. It is based on Rational's efforts to use risk-driven spiral processes and the economics of software development to streamline disciplined software methods. One of the RUP contributors was the CCPDS-R process discussed in Chapter 4. RUP is based on four fundamental tenets: reduce the size or complexity of what needs to be developed, improve the development process, create more proficient teams, and use integrated tools that exploit automation.

Designed to work with UML

RUP defines a four-phase life cycle, each phase of which incorporates multiple iterations or spirals. The phases are Inception, Elaboration, Construction, and Transition. A phase is exited only after the project demonstrates that it has met a phase-specific set of criteria and has developed a reasonable, detailed plan for the next phase. These exit criteria are presented for stakeholder concurrence at a life cycle milestone

Four-phase life cycle with exit criteria and milestones for each phase

review. Appendix D1 provides additional information about these spiral model anchor point milestones.

Comments

Hybrid of agility and discipline

Due to its large volume of process guidelines and "tailor-down" approach, RUP has generally been viewed as a plan-driven, heavy process. Many of the agile attributes are incorporated in the RUP philosophy, but the overall detail of the process has often obscured this. RUP represents one form of hybrid process that incorporates ideas from both the agile and disciplined philosophies. There are two supported versions: RUP Classic and RUP for Small Projects. Rational also provides a RUP Workbench tool and several customization plug-ins, including a plug-in for XP.

Addresses business and economic factors

RUP addresses business workflows and development economic factors that are usually not specifically called out in other methods. The process has been developed to incorporate these factors in both technical and managerial decisions. RUP is currently being extended to address customer economics and return-on-investment considerations.

Tailoring is difficult

RUP is not easy to tailor to many smaller projects. There is a tendency to simply "take it all," which leads to frustration and high implementation costs. The RUP for Small Projects option and evolving tool and plug-ins initiatives aim to provide users with a means to start with a smaller baseline, as well as better tools, guidance, and heuristics for tailoring.

References

Kruchten, P. December 2001. "Agility with the RUP," *Cutter IT Journal,* pp. 27–33 (www.therationaledge.com/content/jan_02).

Kruchten, P. 1999. *The Rational Unified Process (2nd Ed. 2001).* Reading, MA: Addison-Wesley.

Jacobson, I., G. Booch, and J. Rumbaugh. 1999. *The Unified Software Development Process.* Reading, MA: Addison-Wesley.

Royce, W.E. 1998. *Software Project Management: A Unified Framework*. Reading,
MA: Addison-Wesley.
www.rational.com

Team Software Process (TSP)

Levels of Concern	Business Enterprise	Business System	Multiteam Project	Single-Team Project	Individual
		o	o	●	o
Life Cycle Activities	Concept Development	Requirements	Design	Development	Maintenance
		●	o	●	o
Sources of Constraint	Management Processes	Technical Practices	Risk/ Opportunity	Measurement Practices	Customer Interface
	o	o	●	●	o

Thumbnail Sketch

The Team Software Process is designed to support the development of industrial-strength software through the use of teams. Developed by Watts Humphrey at the Software Engineering Institute (SEI), TSP is used in conjunction with the Personal Software Process (PSP). TSP provides a highly detailed template process, based on specific roles and scripts, for selecting, building, and operating a software development team. The process is tailored by the team to meet the project needs and can be more agile in situations of rapid change.

Tailorable, plan-driven development process for teams

TSP objectives aim to build high-performance teams

TSP has five objectives:

1. Build self-directed teams that plan and track their work, establish goals, and own their processes and plans. These can be pure software teams or integrated product teams of 3 to about 20 engineers.
2. Show managers how to coach and motivate their teams and how to help them sustain peak performance.
3. Accelerate software process improvement by making SW-CMM/ CMMI Level 5 behavior normal and expected.
4. Provide improvement guidance to high-maturity organizations.
5. Facilitate university teaching of industrial-grade team skills.

TSP is iterative with relaunches for each iteration

The TSP is an iterative process that begins with a formal Launch event. This four-day meeting establishes the initial project objectives, roles and responsibilities, resource estimates, quality plan, risk management plan, and project processes. It also reviews risks and plans with management. Following an initial phase, usually requirements definition, there are two-day Relaunch events for each successive phase until the project is complete. The Relaunch events define the specific roles and tasks, goals, and quality measures for the following phase.

Comments

TSP tailoring allows matching process to project

TSP has been shown to be very effective in industrial and academic settings. It has a high success rate on early-adopter projects up to about 20 people and, as of this writing, has a 60-person "team of teams" project under way. TSP is a very thoroughly defined process. The educational version, TSPi, includes 21 process scripts, 5 role scripts, and 51 pages of forms. However, the amount of discipline actually used can vary, since the team is responsible for developing their own version of the processes and scripts at the beginning of each cycle of the project. This is essentially "tailoring-down," but, subject to following the

PSP practices and meeting the key exit criteria of the TSP scripts, TSP users can opt for an agile-informed process. In conversations with us, Humphrey indicated that a TSP-trained team could execute the full set of XP practices, perhaps with some small variations, in concert with the PSP/TSP criteria. Of course, this level of self-tailoring would require the team to have a strong complement of Cockburn Levels 2 and 3 experts. The risk-based TSP approach is quite similar to our risk-based approach in Chapter 5. Chapter 3 provides an example of TSP in use.

References

Humphrey, W. 2000. *Introduction to Team Software Process*. Boston: Addison-Wesley.

Humphrey, W. 2002. *Winning with Software*. Boston: Addison-Wesley.

www.sei.cmu.edu

Feature-Driven Development (FDD)

Levels of Concern	Business Enterprise	Business System	Multiteam Project	Single-Team Project	Individual
		o	●	o	o
Life Cycle Activities	Concept Development	Requirements	Design	Development	Maintenance
			●	●	o
Sources of Constraint	Management Processes	Technical Practices	Risk/ Opportunity	Measurement Practices	Customer Interface
	o	●		o	o

Thumbnail Sketch

Processes should support rather than drive

Feature-Driven Development focuses on simple process, efficient modeling, and short, iterative cycles that deliver value to the customer. It grew out of the experiences of Jeff DeLuca and Peter Coad on a complex commercial lending application for a large Singapore bank in 1997–98. FDD depends heavily on good people for domain knowledge, design, and development. A central goal is to have the process in the background to support rather than drive the team.

Five phases— doesn't address requirements elicitation

FDD's five-phase process assumes that the requirements have already been largely captured and are well understood. It proceeds as follows:

1. *Develop an overall model of the product to capture the breadth of the domain.* This is usually described by a class architecture and notes describing the rationale for decisions.
2. *Establish a list of features based on the business needs.* The envisioned product is decomposed from subject area down to business activity, resulting in a list of items that customers find valuable.
3. *Create a development plan based on the list of features.* The continuously refined plan defines the system features and the order of their development.
4. *Develop design packages and work packages for the features assigned to the current iteration.* At this level, features are bundled according to technical reasons rather than business reasons.
5. *Build the features in software.* Implement the classes and methods, inspect the code, test at the unit level, and when complete, integrate into the current build of the overall system.

According to the FDD documentation, Phases 4 and 5 are repeated for each iteration of the project. This would make it no different from an incremental waterfall process. Its agility comes from counting on good people to recognize when it is necessary to backtrack to earlier phases.

FDD differs from XP in two significant ways. Its principle of classes assigned to individuals is the antithesis of XP's collective ownership of code. Its focus on architectures and "getting it right the first time" is the antithesis of XP's simple design and YAGNI. This makes FDD stronger for more stable systems with predictable evolution, more vulnerable to nonpredictable "architecture-breaker" changes.

FDD differs from XP in code ownership and architecture

Comments

Multiple packages may be designed and implemented by several teams, allowing FDD to scale much more easily than some of the other agile methods. The architectural work and planning performed up front provides the structure for parallel development.

Up-front planning and architecture enable multiple concurrent iterations for scaling

FDD emphasizes the importance of good people. It very much needs a strong complement of Cockburn Levels 2 and 3 people to succeed, especially when scaling up. Modifying the architecture during rapid and unpredictable change makes top talent necessary and in general compensates for the lack of explicit focus on risk. While all agile methods generally espouse object-oriented techniques, FDD specifically defines its process and roles with object technology in mind.

Needs good people and strongly coupled to object techniques

References

Coad, P., E. LeFebvre, and J. DeLuca. 2000. *Java Modeling in Color with UML*. Upper Saddle River, NJ: Prentice Hall.

Palmer, S., and J. Felsing. 2002. *A Practical Guide to Feature-Driven Development (The Coad Series)*. Upper Saddle River, NJ: Prentice Hall.

The Coad Letter: www.togethercommunity.com.

Capability Maturity Model Integration (CMMI)

Levels of Concern	Business Enterprise	Business System	Multiteam Project	Single-Team Project	Individual
	o	o	●	●	
Life Cycle Activities	Concept Development	Requirements	Design	Development	Maintenance
	●	●	●	●	●
Sources of Constraint	Management Processes	Technical Practices	Risk/ Opportunity	Measurement Practices	Customer Interface
	o − ●	o	●	●	o

Thumbnail Sketch

Builds on SW-CMM by providing an extensible framework

CMMI represents the latest of the capability maturity models developed by the Software Engineering Institute. It was created to extend process improvement guidance outside of software development, support integration of software and systems engineering, and take advantage of the experience gained from ten years of using the CMM for Software (SW-CMM). As with the SW-CMM, it is light on people factors, because these are covered in a complementary People-CMM.

Includes systems engineering, supplier selection, and IPPD

The CMMI product suite includes models, appraisal methods, training material, technical notes, and application guidance. It primarily covers product development, including the processes associated with software engineering, systems engineering, supplier selection, and integrated process and product development (IPPD).

The models are characterized by a two-dimensional framework—a process requirements dimension defined by Process Areas and a capability improvement dimension defined by Generic Practices. These dimensions are presented in two representations—a continuous set of Process Areas that can be improved individually according to the organization's priorities, and a set of stages that define an ordering of the Process Areas and Generic Practices that is based on experience.

Staged and continuous representations for different process improvement goals

CMMI's integration of software engineering, systems engineering, and integrated product and process development have made it considerably broader and more flexible than SW-CMM. It has added Process Areas such as Integrated Teaming, Requirements Development, and Risk Management that are much more amenable to agile interpretations.

CMMI broader and more flexible than SW-CMM

Comments

The agility of CMMI is difficult to characterize, since as a process improvement reference model it is closer to a set of requirements than a set of practices. That said, we can characterize the processes that are developed to meet those requirements. Generally, CMMI is less restrictive in its requirements than SW-CMM. A liberal reading of the requirements can enable agility. However, if implemented with the general conservatism and heavyweight maturity assessments traditionally afforded SW-CMM, CMMI-compliant processes will be heavyweight and strongly plan-driven. More information may be found in Appendix C.

CMMI is a reference model, not a method

References

Chrissis, M., M. Konrad, and S. Shrum. 2003. *CMMI: Guidelines for Process Integration and Product Improvement.* Boston: Addison-Wesley.

Ahern, D., A. Clouse, and R. Turner. 2001. *CMMI Distilled: A Practical Introduction to Integrated Process Improvement (2nd Ed. 2003).* Boston: Addison-Wesley.

www.sei.cmu.edu

Capability Maturity Model for Software (SW-CMM)

Levels of Concern	Business Enterprise	Business System	Multiteam Project	Single-Team Project	Individual
	o		●	●	
Life Cycle Activities	Concept Development	Requirements	Design	Development	Maintenance
		o	●	●	●
Sources of Constraint	Management Processes	Technical Practices	Risk/ Opportunity	Measurement Practices	Customer Interface
	●	o	o	●	o

Thumbnail Sketch

SW-CMM began as quality checklist

SW-CMM development was coordinated by a team led by Watts Humphrey at the Software Engineering Institute at Carnegie-Mellon University and is based on the quality work of Deming, Juran, and Crosby. It was created in response to the U.S. Air Force's desire for a way to evaluate the companies that developed their software. Beginning as a checklist, SW-CMM evolved into a roadmap for maturing software development processes. It is fundamentally a management model with only one part devoted to technical software development practices. It is light on people factors because they are covered in a complementary People-CMM.

Five levels of maturity

The SW-CMM defines five successively increasing levels of organizational maturity. Each level is characterized by a set of Key Process Areas (KPAs) that define specific goals, practices, abilities, and artifacts. It is from SW-CMM that we get the concept of a "Level *n* organization" that is often referred to in supplier source selections. If an organization is appraised by an independent organization and is determined to have met all the goals and practices of the KPAs in a particular level, as well as those in all of the preceding levels, it can be said to have "achieved" that level. SW-CMM includes assessment methods and a training infrastructure coordinated by SEI.

Comments

The goals of SW-CMM Level 5 are similar to some of the agile tenets concerning continuous improvement. Unfortunately, most organizations don't reach Level 5 so SW-CMM application generally results in fairly heavyweight plan-driven organizations.

SW-CMM usually results in heavyweight processes

SW-CMM has had a significant impact on software development by focusing on the processes that are crucial to successful development. It gathered a large body of knowledge based on successful projects and presented it in a way that was effective for the practitioners and easy for management to deploy and measure. However, SW-CMM's view of software development as being based on a stable set of predefined requirements creates major problems in applying it within rapidly changing environments where requirements are more emergent.

Has had a significant impact on software development

References

Humphrey, W. 1989. *Managing the Software Process*. Reading, MA: Addison-Wesley.

Paulk, M., et al. 1995. *The Capability Maturity Model: Guidelines for Improving the Software Process*. Reading, MA: Addison-Wesley.

www.sei.cmu.edu

Personal Software Process (PSP)

Levels of Concern	Business Enterprise	Business System	Multiteam Project	Single-Team Project	Individual
					●
Life Cycle Activities	Concept Development	Requirements	Design	Development	Maintenance
			o	●	
Sources of Constraint	Management Processes	Technical Practices	Risk/ Opportunity	Measurement Practices	Customer Interface
	●	o		●	

Thumbnail Sketch

Focuses on software development by individuals

PSP—along with Team Software Process—was developed by Watts Humphrey to provide the "how" that relates to the SW-CMM's "what" at the individual-programmer level. As such, PSP and TSP are much closer to the practitioner level of the agile methods than the organizationally focused CMMs.

Improves individual programming skills

PSP is directed toward improving individual programming skills. Humphrey describes it as "a structured framework of forms, guidelines, and procedures for developing software." It applies the general quality approaches that inform the SW-CMM to the way in which individuals plan, execute, measure, and improve their programming activities.

Four levels of improvement

PSP is based on four levels of personal process—PSP Levels 0 through 3. The software engineer learning PSP begins by establishing a personal baseline using basic measurements and reports (PSP0). This level is improved by adding a coding standard, a size measurement, and the development of a personal process improvement proposal (PSP0.1). The second level adds planning (through size estimation based on the measurements of PSP0.1) and a disciplined approach to testing (PSP1). Enhancements to this level include task and schedule planning (PSP1.1). The third PSP level is centered around quality and introduces code and design reviews (PSP2.0). It is extended with the introduction of design templates (PSP2.1). The final level (PSP3) sets the programmer on a cyclical development and improvement cycle.

Comments

PSP is nonprescriptive about specific programming methodologies and focuses on build-to-specification programming. It is highly effective as a programming equivalent to biofeedback, by making one's unconscious programming bad habits perceptible and subject to conscious mental control. PSP has demonstrated its effectiveness in academic and industrial venues. Some people find PSP's attention to self-monitoring relatively easy and valuable to continue, while others do not.

Effective, but concerns about long-term impacts

References

Humphrey, W. 1995. *A Discipline for Software Engineering: The Complete PSP Book.* Reading, MA: Addison-Wesley.

Humphrey, W. 1997. *Introduction to the Personal Software Process.* Reading, MA: Addison-Wesley.

Cleanroom

Levels of Concern	Business Enterprise	Business System	Multiteam Project	Single-Team Project	Individual
			o	●	●
Life Cycle Activities	Concept Development	Requirements	Design	Development	Maintenance
		o	●	●	o
Sources of Constraint	Management Processes	Technical Practices	Risk/ Opportunity	Measurement Practices	Customer Interface
	●	●		●	o

Thumbnail Sketch

Mathematically based, highly disciplined method

Cleanroom software engineering was developed by Harlan Mills at IBM. It uses mathematically based verification to develop software with certified reliability. It is based on the concept that a computer program is a complex mathematical function, and that its desired operation can be precisely specified. The name "Cleanroom" comes from the precision electronics world, where a physical clean room prevents introduction of defects during production.

Focus is on defect-free code

The entire Cleanroom approach is focused on defect-free code. Stringent reviews of design and code are conducted before the first compilation, and defect measures are maintained from that point forward. System testing is based on probabilistic estimates of functional usage.

Complete discipline

Cleanroom is a complete software development discipline including processes for planning, specification, design, verification, coding, testing, and certifying software. The approach is incremental in nature.

Initially, the system behavior is specified as a "black box" in terms of stimuli, responses, and transition rules. From this black box, the team performs a stepwise refinement according to strict construction rules. The end result is a "clear box" that contains procedural information. Tools have been built to support cleanroom processes, particularly statistical testing.

Comments

Cleanroom requires highly skilled practitioners. It exhibited a number of successes with early adopters, but has been difficult to scale up or use in highly dynamic environments. Because of this, its use has declined. When there is a need for highly reliable software, and there are skilled and trained practitioners available, Cleanroom is usually worth the effort. Some of its practices, such as statistical testing, can be effectively used elsewhere.

Difficult, but worth the effort for highly reliable software requirements

References

Prowell, S., et al. 1999. *Cleanroom Software Engineering: Technology and Process.* Reading, MA: Addison-Wesley.

Becker, S., and J. Whittaker. 1997. *Cleanroom Software Engineering Practices (4th Ed.).* Idea Group Publishing Co.

Method Comparison Table

This table combines the profile ratings of the methods described in the appendix into a single table. For clarity, the black dots are replaced by black squares and the open dots by gray squares. Where there is a range of values, the square is striped.

Method	Levels of Concern					Life Cycle Coverage					Sources of Constraint				
	Business Enterprise	Business System	Multi-team Project	Single-team Project	Individual	Concept Development	Requirements	Design	Development	Maintenance	Management Processes	Technical Practices	Risk/Opportuinty	Measurement Practices	Customer Interface
Scrum		▨	▨	▨	▨	▨	▨	▨	▨	▨	■		▨		▨
ASD	▨	▨	▨	▨		▨	▨	▨	▨	▨	▨		■		▨
Lean Dev	▨	■				▨		▨		▨	▥		■		
Crystal			■	■	▨	▨	▨	▨	▨	▨	▥	■	■		▥
XP		▨	▨	■			■	■	■	■	■	■		▨	■
DSDM	▨	■	■	■		▨	▨	▨	▨	▨	■	▨	■		■
RUP		▨	■	■		▨	▨	▨	▨	▨	■	■	■	▨	■
TSP		▨	▨	■	▨		▨	▨	■		■	■	■	■	▨
FDD			■	■		▨	▨	■	■		■		■	■	■
CMMI	▨	■	■	▨		■	■	■	■	■	▥	■	■	■	■
SW-CMM	▨		■	■		▨	▨	■	■	■	■	▨	■	■	■
PSP					■	▨	▨	■	■		■	■		■	
Cleanroom			▨	■	■		▨	▨	▨	▨	■	■		■	▨

Appendix B

Manifesto for Agile
Software Development

We are uncovering better ways of developing software by doing it and helping others do it. Through this work we have come to value:

- **Individuals and interactions** over processes and tools.
- **Working software** over comprehensive documentation.
- **Customer collaboration** over contract negotiation.
- **Responding to change** over following a plan.

That is, while there is value in the items on the right, we value the items on the left more.

Kent Beck	James Grenning	Robert C. Martin
Mike Beedle	Jim Highsmith	Steve Mellor
Arie van Bennekum	Andrew Hunt	Ken Schwaber
Alistair Cockburn	Ron Jeffries	Jeff Sutherland
Ward Cunningham	Jon Kern	Dave Thomas
Martin Fowler	Brian Marick	

Principles behind the Agile Manifesto

We follow these principles:

1. Our highest priority is to satisfy the customer through early and continuous delivery of valuable software.
2. Welcome changing requirements, even late in development. Agile processes harness change for the customer's competitive advantage.
3. Deliver working software frequently, from a couple of weeks to a couple of months, with a preference to the shorter timescale.
4. Business people and developers must work together daily throughout the project.
5. Build projects around motivated individuals. Give them the environment and support they need, and trust them to get the job done.
6. The most efficient and effective method of conveying information to and within a development team is face-to-face conversation.
7. Working software is the primary measure of progress.
8. Agile processes promote sustainable development. The sponsors, developers, and users should be able to maintain a constant pace indefinitely.
9. Continuous attention to technical excellence and good design enhances agility.
10. Simplicity—the art of maximizing the amount of work not done—is essential.
11. The best architectures, requirements, and designs emerge from self-organizing teams.
12. At regular intervals, the team reflects on how to become more effective, then tunes and adjusts its behavior accordingly.

Appendix C

Capability Maturity Models

This appendix is a primer on the Capability Maturity Models (CMMs), their development and use. It is not intended to be complete or exhaustive, but to provide sufficient understanding for reading and using this book.

A Short History of CMMs

The development of the Capability Maturity Model for Software (SW-CMM) formally began in 1986 as a collaboration between the Software Engineering Institute (SEI) of Carnegie-Mellon University and the MITRE Corporation. Based on earlier work at IBM, the goal was to produce a framework for the U.S. federal government to assess the capabilities of its contractors in the area of software development. In 1987, a team led by Watts Humphrey published an initial framework and a maturity questionnaire. By 1991 the concept had evolved into Version 1.0 of the SW-CMM.[1] In 1993, an improved Version 1.1 was released[2] and subsequently published in book form.[3]

The SW-CMM slowly gained momentum as a guide for improving software development capability. The Department of Defense aided that growth by using CMM process maturity level as an exclusion criterion for awarding many of its largest software acquisition contracts.

At the same time, the International Standards Organization (ISO) was also working on software process and developed two standards, 15504 and 12207. These standards covered much of the same material as the SW-CMM, but used a different architecture for describing the processes and their requirements. Complicating the issue was the development of additional CMMs or CMM-like structures for systems engineering, security, personnel, and other disciplines.

In 1997, the multiple-model situation led to the Capability Maturity Model Integration (CMMI) effort, cosponsored by the Department of Defense and the National Defense Industrial Association. CMMI's goal was to establish a single, extensible framework that would provide a standard for CMMs, incorporate new understanding of development practice, and attempt to harmonize with the ISO standards. The result was the release of the CMMI Version 1.1 product suite in 2001.[4, 5, 6]

CMM Concepts

Fundamentally, a CMM is an organized set of practices which, when applied diligently within an organization, will improve its process capability in one or more discipline areas such as software or systems engineering. Process capability is defined as the inherent ability of a process to produce planned results. As the capability of each process is improved, it becomes predictable and measurable, and the most significant causes of poor quality and productivity are controlled or eliminated.

SW-CMM sets the requirements in a framework of Key Process Areas (KPAs) and Maturity Levels 2–5. Level 1 is assumed to be the normal chaotic state of immature organizational processes. KPAs describe the minimum activities and common features of a process for a particular area. Each Maturity Level consists of a number of KPAs. The ordering of the levels is based on the experiences of successful projects as to what to improve first. Situation-based optimization at Level 5 means that an agile home ground organization would optimize around agility. A plan-driven home ground organization would optimize around more prescient planning and control. Table C-1 shows the structure of the SW-CMM.

CMMI extends the SW-CMM concept. It is essentially a set of requirements for engineering processes, particularly those involved in product development. It consists of two kinds of information—Process Areas (PAs) that describe the goals and activities that make up process requirements in a specific focus area, and Generic Practices (GPs) that are applied across the Process Areas to guide improvement in process capability.

The PAs, which roughly coincide with the SW-CMM KPAs, include requirements for:

- Basic project management and control
- Basic engineering life cycle processes
- Fundamental support processes
- Process monitoring and improvement processes (similar to SW-CMM)
- Integrated development using teams

The second type of information CMMI provides is a set of Generic Practices that support the improvement of the processes established under the Process Areas. The Generic Practices are associated with a six-level capability scale that describes relative capabilities as follows:

- Not performed (not even doing the basics)
- Performed (just doing it)

Table C-1 Summary of SW-CMM		
Maturity Level	**Focus**	**Key Process Areas**
5. Optimizing	Continual process improvement; Situation-based optimization	Defect prevention Technology change management Process change management
4. Managed	Product and process quality; Manage by measures	Quantitative process management Software quality management
3. Defined	Engineering processes and organizational support; Standard processes	Organization process focus Organization process definition Training program Integrated software management Software product engineering Intergroup coordination Peer reviews
2. Repeatable	Project management processes; Tame local chaos	Requirements management Software project planning Software project tracking and oversight Software subcontract management Software quality assurance Software configuration management
1. Initial	Competent people (and heroics); chaotic	None

- Managed (fundamental infrastructure to accomplish the process generally at the project level)
- Defined (institutionalizes a standard version of the process for tailoring by projects)
- Quantitatively managed process (uses quantitative measures to monitor and control selected subprocesses)
- Optimizing (constant adaptation of processes based on quantitative measures)

CMMI can be viewed in two representations: staged (Process Areas are organized by maturity levels, like the SW-CMM) and continuous (Process Areas are evaluated and improved separately, similar to the ISO/Spice work[7]). For easier comparison to the SW-CMM, we use the staged representation in Table C-2 to illustrate the CMMI structure.

Using Models to Improve Processes

Models provide a common framework and vocabulary to support organizations to improve their processes. Generally, an organization is assessed against some or all of the model to establish a baseline. The number of practices that are satisfied are identified and action plans established to develop unimplemented or insufficient practices. The plans are executed, and the cycle repeats with further appraisals to measure progress and achievement, which result in new action plans and so forth.

The fundamental idea is that as the organization establishes common processes, trains its personnel, and begins to measure the performance of its processes, it will better understand and then focus in on those processes critical to its business and continuously improve them. This results in a minimal set of very efficient processes that can be closely monitored for performance within expected ranges.

Table C-2 CMMI Structure (Staged)		
Level	**Focus**	**Process Areas**
5. Optimizing	*Continuous process improvement*	Organizational Innovation and Deployment
		Causal Analysis and Resolution
4. Quantitatively Managed	*Quantitative management*	Organizational Process Performance
		Quantitative Project Management
3. Defined	*Process standardization*	Requirements Development
		Technical Solution
		Product Integration (SS)
		Verification
		Validation
		Organizational Process Focus
		Organizational Process Definition
		Organizational Training
		Integrated Project Management
		Integrated Supplier Management
		Risk Management
		Decision Analysis and Resolution
		Organizational Environment for Integration *(IPPD)*
		Integrated Teaming *(IPPD)*

Level	Focus	Process Areas
2. Managed	*Basic project management*	Requirements Management
		Project Planning
		Project Monitoring and Control
		Supplier Agreement Management
		Measurement and Analysis
		Process and Product Quality Assurance
		Configuration Management
1. Performed		

The CMMI has added several Process Areas not in the SW-CMM that encourage agility and customer collaboration, including Integrated Teaming, Requirements Development, and Risk Management. These additions make it easier to accommodate agile methods within the CMMI framework than within the SW-CMM framework.

Appendix D

Tools for Balancing

D1. The Spiral Model Anchor Point Milestones

The spiral model anchor point milestones were initially developed in a series of workshops by the USC Center for Software Engineering and its government and industrial affiliates. They addressed two primary problems:

1. The lack of well-defined milestones for evaluating and tracking progress while using the spiral development model.
2. The need for a set of common commitment points to use as the phase boundaries for the COCOMO II cost and schedule estimation model.

The milestone content and rationale were initially documented in 1996.[1] They were subsequently adopted as the phase gates in the Rational Unified Process,[2, 3, 4] the USC Win Win Spiral and MBASE process models,[5, 6] and the organization-level CeBASE Method.[7]

The specific content of the first two anchor point milestones are summarized in Table D-1. They include increasingly detailed, risk-driven definitions of the system's operational concept, prototypes, requirements, architectures, life cycle plan, and feasibility rationale. For the feasibility rationale, the results of prototypes, simulations, models, benchmarks,

Table D-1 LCO and LCA Anchor Points

Milestone Element	Life Cycle Objectives (LCO)	Life Cycle Architecture (LCA)
Definition of Operational Concept	Top-level system objectives and scope —System boundary —Environment parameters and assumptions —Evolution parameters Operational concept	Elaboration of system objectives and scope by increment Elaboration of operational concept by increment
System Prototype(s)	Exercise key usage scenarios Resolve critical risks	Exercise range of usage scenarios Resolve major outstanding risks
Definition of System Requirements	Top-level functions, interfaces, quality attribute levels, including: —Growth vectors —Priorities Stakeholders' concurrence on essentials	Elaboration of functions, interfaces, quality attributes by increment —Identification of TBDs (to-be-determined items) Stakeholders' concurrence on their priority concerns
Definition of System and Software Architecture	Top-level definition of at least one feasible architecture —Physical and logical elements and relationships —Choices of COTS and reusable software elements Identification of infeasible architecture options	Choice of architecture and elaboration by increment —Physical and logical components, connectors, configurations, constraints —COTS, reuse choices —Domain-architecture and architectural style choices Architecture evolution parameters
Definition of Life Cycle Plan	Identification of life cycle stakeholders —Users, customers, developers, maintainers, interpreters, general public, others Identification of life cycle process model —Top-level stages, increments Top-level WWWWWHH* by stage	Elaboration of WWWWWHH* for Initial Operational Capability (IOC) —Partial elaboration, identification of key TBDs for later increments

Milestone Element	Life Cycle Objectives (LCO)	Life Cycle Architecture (LCA)
Feasibility Rationale	Assurance of consistency among elements above —Via analysis, measurement, prototyping, simulation, etc. —Business case analysis for requirements, feasible architectures	Assurance of consistency among elements above All major risks resolved or covered by risk management plan
Notes: Risk-driven level of detail at each milestone *WWWWWHH: Why, What, When, Who, Where, How, How much		

and analyses are presented to verify that the milestone elements constitute a consistent and feasible system definition.

The first milestone is the Life Cycle Objectives (LCO) milestone, at which management verifies the basis for a business commitment to proceed at least through an architecting stage. This involves verifying that there is at least one system architecture and choice of COTS/reuse components that is shown to be feasible to implement within budget and schedule constraints, to satisfy key stakeholder win conditions, and to generate a viable investment business case.

The second milestone is the Life Cycle Architecture (LCA) milestone, at which management verifies the basis for a sound commitment to product development and evolution (a particular system architecture with specific COTS and reuse commitments that is shown to be feasible with respect to budget, schedule, requirements, operations concept and business case, identification and commitment of all key life cycle stakeholders, and elimination of all critical risk items). The AT&T/Lucent Architecture Review Board technique[8] is an excellent management review approach involving the LCO and LCA milestones. It is similar to the recent, highly successful DoD best practice of software Independent Expert Program Reviews.[9]

The third anchor point is the system's Initial Operational Capability (IOC).[10] There are many possible minor milestones (adjusted to the particular project as needed) that may lie between LCO and IOC and several important postdeployment milestones beyond IOC.

Table D-2 summarizes the pass/fail criteria for the LCO, LCA, and IOC anchor points.

The focus of the LCO review is to ensure that at least one architecture choice is viable from a business perspective. The focus of the LCA review is to commit to a single detailed definition of the review artifacts. The project must have either eliminated all significant risks or put in place an acceptable risk management plan. The focus of the IOC review, also called the Transition Readiness Review, is to ensure that the initial users, operators, and maintainers (generally equivalent to beta testers) are fully prepared to successfully operate the delivered system. If the pass/fail criteria for any review are not satisfied, the package should be reworked.

The anchor point milestones work well as common commitment points across commercial, aerospace, and government organizations and across a variety of process model variants because they reflect similar commitment points during one's lifetime.

The LCO milestone is the equivalent of getting engaged, and the LCA milestone is the equivalent of getting married. As in life, if you marry your architecture in haste, you and your stakeholders will repent at leisure (if, in Internet time, any leisure time is available). The third

Table D-2 LCO, LCA, and IOC Pass/Fail Criteria

LCO	LCA	IOC
For at least one architecture, a system built to that architecture will: • Support the core Operational Concept • Satisfy the core Requirements • Be faithful to the Prototype(s) • Be buildable within the budgets and schedules in the plan • Show a viable business case • Have its key stakeholders committed to support the Elaboration Phase (to LCA)	For a specific detailed architecture, a system built to that architecture will: • Support the elaborated Operational Concept • Satisfy the elaborated Requirements • Be faithful to the Prototype(s) • Be buildable within the budgets and schedules in the plan • Have all major risks resolved or covered by a risk management plan • Have its key stakeholders committed to support the full life cycle	An implemented architecture, an operational system that has: • Realized the Operational Concept • Implemented the initial operational requirements • Prepared a system operation and support plan • Prepared the initial site(s) in which the system will be deployed for transition • Prepared the users, operators, and maintainers to assume their operational roles

anchor point milestone, the Initial Operational Capability, constitutes an even larger commitment: It is the equivalent of having your first child, with all the associated commitments of care and feeding of a legacy system.

D2. Benefits Realization Analysis and the DMR Results Chain

Benefits Realized

Many software projects fail by succumbing to the "Field of Dreams" syndrome. This refers to the American movie in which a Midwestern farmer has a dream that if he builds a baseball field on his farm, the legendary players of the past will appear and play on it ("If you build it, they will come").

In *The Information Paradox,*[11] John Thorp discusses the paradox that organizations' success in profitability or market capitalization does not correlate with their level of investment in information technology (IT). He traces this paradox to an IT and software analogy of the "Field of Dreams" syndrome: "Build the software and the benefits will come."

To counter this syndrome, Thorp and his company, the DMR Consulting Group, have developed a Benefits Realization Approach (BRA) for determining and coordinating the other initiatives besides software and IT system development that are needed in order for the organization to realize the potential IT system benefits. The most significant of the BRA techniques, the Results Chain, is discussed next.

Results Chain

Figure D-1 shows a simple Results Chain provided as an example in *The Information Paradox.* It establishes a framework linking Initiatives that consume resources (e.g., implement a new order entry system for sales) to Contributions (not delivered systems, but their effects on existing operations) and Outcomes, which may lead either to further contributions or to added value (e.g., increased sales). A particularly important contribution of the Results Chain is the link to Assumptions, which condition the realization of the Outcomes. Thus, in Figure D-1, if order-to-delivery time turns out not to be an important buying criterion for the product being sold (e.g., for stockable commodities such as soap and pencils), the reduced time to deliver the product will not result in increased sales.

The Results Chain is a valuable framework by which software project members can work with their clients to identify additional nonsoftware

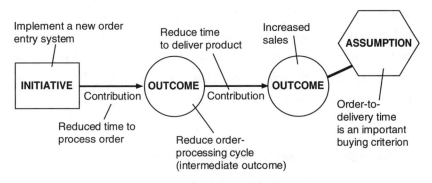

Figure D-1   Benefits Realization Approach Results Chain

initiatives that may be needed to realize the potential benefits enabled by the software/IT system initiative. These may also identify some additional success-critical stakeholders who need to be represented and to "buy into" the shared vision.

For example, the initiative to implement a new order entry system may reduce the time required to process orders only if some additional initiatives or system features are pursued to convince the salespeople that the new system will be good for their careers and to train them in how to use the system effectively. For example, if the order entry system is so efficiency-optimized that it doesn't keep track of sales credits, the salespeople will fight using it.

Further, the reduced order processing cycle will reduce the time to deliver products only if additional initiatives are pursued to coordinate the order entry system with the order fulfillment system. Some classic cases where this didn't happen were the late deliveries of Hershey's Halloween candy and Toys 'R' Us Christmas toys.

Such additional initiatives need to be added to the Results Chain. Besides increasing its realism, this also identifies additional success-critical stakeholders (salespeople and order fulfillment people) who need to be involved in the system definition and development process. The expanded Results Chain involves these stakeholders not just in a stovepipe software project to satisfy some requirements, but in a *program* of related software and nonsoftware initiatives focused on value-producing end results.

D3. Schedule as an Independent Variable

The Schedule as Independent Variable (SAIV) process model is a scalable, architecture-driven version of the timeboxing approach.[12] It is a special case of the risk-driven spiral model, to be used when the risk of meeting an ambitious schedule is a top-priority concern. Counterpart versions can be used for Cost or Schedule-Cost-Quality as Independent Variable processes. Over the last seven years, the SAIV model has been used on over 50 e-service projects at USC, with a 92 percent success rate of on-time, client-satisfactory delivery.

The SAIV process model consists of six major steps:

1. Shared vision and expectations management
2. Feature prioritization
3. Schedule range estimation
4. Architecture and core capabilities determination
5. Incremental development
6. Change and progress monitoring and control

Shared Vision and Expectations Management

As graphically described in *Death March,*[13] many software projects lose the opportunity to assure a rapid, on-time delivery by inflating client expectations and overpromising on delivered capabilities. The first step in the SAIV process model is to avoid this by obtaining stakeholder agreement that meeting a fixed schedule for delivering the system's Initial Operational Capability is the most critical objective, and that the other objectives such as the IOC feature content can be variable, subject to meeting acceptable levels of quality and post-IOC scalability.

Often, the customers and developers have unrealistic expectations about what is easy or hard for each other to do. We have found that providing them with lists of developer and client "simplifiers and complicators" improves their ability to converge on a realistic set of expectations for the delivered system.[14] The resulting shared vision enables the stakeholders to rapidly renegotiate the requirements as they encounter changing conditions.

Feature Prioritization

Feature prioritization can be negotiated among stakeholders in several manual or tool-aided ways. The USC e-services projects use the USC/GroupSystems.com EasyWinWin requirements negotiation tool to converge on a mutually satisfactory (win-win) set of project requirements.[15] One step in this process involves the stakeholders prioritizing the requirements by assessing their relative importance and difficulty, each on a scale of 0 to 10. This process is carried out in parallel with initial system prototyping, which helps ensure that the priority assessments are realistic.

Schedule Range Estimation

The developers then use a mix of expert judgment and parametric cost modeling to determine how many of the top-priority features can be developed in 24 weeks under optimistic and pessimistic assumptions. For the parametric model, the USC e-services projects use COCOMO II, which estimates 90 percent confidence limits on both cost and schedule,[16] and an analogy-based Agile COCOMO II version. Other models provide similar capabilities.

Architecture and Core Capability Determination

The most serious mistake a project can make at this point is just to pick the topmost-priority features with 90 percent confidence of being developed in 24 weeks. This can cause two main problems: producing an IOC with an incoherent and incompatible set of features; and delivering these without an underlying architecture supporting easy scalability up to the full feature set and workload.

First, the core capability must be selected so that its features add up to a coherent and workable end-to-end operational capability. Second, the remainder of the lower-priority IOC requirements and subsequent evolution requirements must be used in determining a system architecture facilitating evolution to full operational capability. Still the best approach for achieving this is to encapsulate the foreseeable sources of change within modules.[17] As discussed in Chapters 4 and 5, smaller projects can often use simple design and timeboxing instead, but larger projects increasingly need architectural support.

Incremental Development

Since the core capability has only a 90 percent assurance of being completed in 24 weeks, this means that about 10 percent of the time, the project will just be able to deliver the core capabilities in 24 weeks, perhaps with some extra effort or occasionally by further reducing the top-priority feature set. In the most likely case, however, the project will achieve its core capability with about 20 to 30 percent of the schedule remaining. This time can then be used to add the next-highest priority features into the IOC (again, assuming that the system has been architected to facilitate this).

An important step at this point is to provide the operational stakeholders (users, operators, maintainers) with a Core Capability Drivethrough.

Often, this is the first point at which the realities of actually taking delivery of and living with the new system hit home for the users, and their priorities for the remaining capabilities may change.

Also, this is an excellent point for the stakeholders to reconfirm the likely final IOC content and to synchronize plans for conversion, training, installation, and cutover from current operations to the new IOC.

Change and Progress Monitoring and Control

As progress is being monitored with respect to plans, there are three major sources of change, which may require revaluation and modification of the project's plans:

1. *Schedule slips.* Traditionally, these can happen because of unforeseen technical difficulties, staffing difficulties, customer or supplier delays, and so on.
2. *Requirements changes.* These may include changes in priorities, changes in current requirements, or needs for new high-priority requirements.
3. *Project changes.* These may include budget cuts, staffing changes, COTS changes, or new marketing-related tasks (e.g., interim sponsor demos).

In some cases, these changes can be accommodated within the existing plans. If not, there is a need to rapidly renegotiate and restructure the plans. If this involves the addition of new tasks on the project's critical path, some other tasks on the critical path must be reduced or eliminated. There are several options for doing this, including dropping or deferring lower-priority features, reusing existing software, or adding expert personnel. In no cases should new critical-path tasks be added without adjustments in the delivery schedule.

Appendix E

Empirical Information

This appendix contains information about how the costs and benefits of agile and plan-driven methods can be and have been measured. Unfortunately, since agile methods are relatively recent developments, relatively little agile data is available.

Some of the information uses existing models, like COCOMO II, to infer how agile and plan-driven approaches work based on historical data. Others present experimental findings.

We hope that this collection of material will provide the basis for further work in quantifying the costs and benefits associated with software development practices: agile, plan-driven, and hybrid.

E1. The Cost of Change: Empirical Findings

Figure E-1, from Kent Beck's *Extreme Programming Explained*,[1] is "the technical premise for XP." If the cost of making a software change "rose slowly over time . . . you would make decisions as late in the process as possible . . . and . . . only implement what you need to."

However, "If a flattened cost curve makes XP possible, a steep change cost curve makes XP impossible." This conclusion is largely borne out

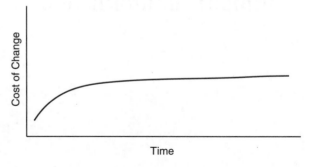

Figure E-1   The Cost of Change May Not Rise Dramatically over Time.

by a real-options economic analysis of XP under these comparative conditions.[2]

The steep version of the cost-of-change curve was discovered by several organizations in the 1970s (TRW, IBM, Bell Labs Safeguard). They found rather consistently that a postdelivery software change was about 100 times as expensive as a Requirements-phase software change. A summary of these and other results in the 1981 book *Software Engineering Economics*[3] found that while the 100:1 figure was generally true for large systems, a 5:1 figure was more characteristic of smaller systems (2 to 5 KSLOC).

Considerable uncertainty has arisen over whether these escalation factors remain representative in today's software development environment. To explore this and related questions, the National Science Foundation–sponsored Center for Empirically Based Software Engineering (CeBASE), formed by the University of Maryland and the University of Southern California, performed a literature search and held three e-Workshops involving people with relevant experience and data.[4] The results tended to confirm the 100:1 ratio for large projects, with factors of 117:1 and 137:1 recorded, and a 1996 survey showed a range of

70–125:1.[5] However, related e-Workshop discussions indicated that change costs tended to have a Pareto distribution, with 80 percent of the cost-to-change coming from the 20 percent of the changes with the most system-wide impact. Several participants indicated that the cost of the "expensive 20 percent" changes can be significantly reduced for large systems by investments in early risk reduction and architecting to localize change effects—effectively a Big Design Up Front (BDUF). A major success story in this regard—and the only project to our knowledge with experience data to match Figure E-1—is the million-line CCPDS-R project we describe in Chapter 4. In general, large projects tend to have steep cost-to-change curves and do not look like good candidates for XP.

Although Beck and others have provided anecdotal data on agile change experiences fitting Figure E-1, no empirical data was found for small, agile projects. Fortunately, a recent summary of two small commercial Java projects mostly following some XP practices (pair programming, test first, on-site customer), and compliant with the remaining XP practices, does provide empirical data on agile cost-of-change as shown in Figures E-2 and E-3.[6]

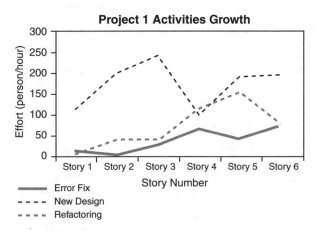

Figure E-2   Project 1 Cost-of-Change Growth

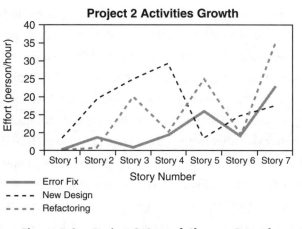

Figure E-3   Project 2 Cost-of-Change Growth

No data was available on the number of changes and the effort per change, but the percentage of total story development effort by story number for Project 1 shows an average increase from one story to the next of about 6 percent per story number for refactoring effort, and about 4 percent per story for error fix effort. The corresponding figures for Project 2 are 5 percent and 3 percent. These are nontrivial rates of increase, and while clearly not as good as the anecdotal experiences of agile experts, they are more likely representative of mainstream XP experience. The small decrease in rates from Project 1 to Project 2 indicates there was a small, but not dominant, XP learning curve effect. Reifer's 2002 survey[7] cites some proprietary empirical data with similar characteristics.

E2. How Much Architecting Is Enough? A COCOMO II Analysis

We have shown several qualitative analyses in Chapter 5 indicating that one can balance the risks of having too little project discipline with the risks of having too much project discipline, to find a "sweet spot" operating point that minimizes the overall risk exposure for a given project.

We have shown qualitatively that as a project's size and criticality increase, the sweet spot moves toward more project discipline, and vice versa.

However, these results would have stronger credibility if shown to be true for a quantitative analysis backed up by a critical mass of data. Here we show the results of such a quantitative analysis, based on the cost estimating relationships in the COCOMO II cost estimation model and its calibration to 161 diverse project data points.[8] The projects in the COCOMO II database include management information systems, electronic services, telecommunications, middleware, engineering and science, command and control, and realtime process control software projects. Their sizes range from 2.6 KSLOC to 1,300 KSLOC, with 13 projects below 10 KSLOC and 5 projects above 1,000 KSLOC.

The risk-balancing analysis is based on one of the calibrated COCOMO II scale factors, Architecture and Risk Resolution, called RESL in the COCOMO II model. Calibrating the RESL scale factor was a test of the hypothesis that proceeding into software development with inadequate architecture and risk resolution results would cause project effort to increase (due to the software rework necessary to overcome the architecture deficiencies and to resolve the risks late in the development cycle), and that the rework effort increase percentage would be larger for larger projects.

The regression analysis to calibrate the RESL factor and the other 22 COCOMO II cost drivers confirmed this hypothesis with a statistically significant result. The calibration results determined that for this sample of projects, the difference between a Very Low RESL rating (corresponding to an architecting investment of 5 percent of the development time) and an Extra High rating (corresponding to an investment of over 40 percent, here established at 50 percent) was an extra 7.07 percent added to the exponent relating project effort to product size. This translates to an extra 18 percent effort for a small, 10 KSLOC project, and an extra 91 percent effort for an extra-large, 10,000 KSLOC project.

The full set of effects for each of the RESL rating levels and corresponding architecting investment percentages are shown in Table E-1 for projects of sizes 10, 100, and 10,000 KSLOC. Also shown are the corresponding total delay in delivery percentages, obtained by adding the architecting investment time to the rework time, assuming a constant team size during rework to translate added effort into added schedule. Thus, in the bottom two rows of Table E-1, we can see that added investments in architecture definition and risk resolution are more than repaid by savings in rework time for a 10,000 KSLOC project up to an investment of 33 percent, after which the total delay percentage increases.

This identifies the minimum-delay architecting investment "sweet spot" for a 10,000 KSLOC project to be around 33 percent. Figure E-4 shows the results of Table E-1 graphically. It indicates that for a 10,000 KSLOC project, the sweet spot is actually a flat region around a 37 percent architecting investment. For a 100 KSLOC project, the sweet spot is a flat region around 20 percent. For a 10 KSLOC project, the sweet spot is at around a 5 percent investment in architecting. The term "architecting" is taken from Rechtin's *System Architecting* book,[9] in which it includes the overall concurrent effort involved in developing and documenting a system's operational concept, requirements, architecture, and life cycle strategic plan. It is roughly equivalent to the agilists' term Big Design Up Front.[10] Thus, the results in Table E-1 and Figure E-1 confirm that investments in architecting and BDUF are minimally necessary for small projects, but increasingly necessary as the project size increases.

Table E-1 Effect of Architecting Investment Level on Total Project Delay

COCOMO II RESL Rating	Very Low	Low	Nominal	High	Very High	Extra High
% Architecting Investment	5	10	17	25	33	>40 (50)
Scale Factor Exponent for Rework Effort	1.0707	1.0565	1.0424	1.0283	1.0141	1.0000
10 KSLOC Project: Added Rework %	18	14	10	7	3	0
Project Delay %	23	24	27	32	36	50
100 KSLOC Project: Added Rework %	38	30	21	14	7	0
Project Delay %	43	40	38	39	40	50
10,000 KSLOC Project: Added Rework %	91	68	48	30	14	0
Project Delay %	96	78	65	55	47	50

A couple of caveats are worth mentioning about the analysis, however. It assumes a low level of requirements volatility. If the requirements on the 10,000 KSLOC project were highly volatile, the architecting documentation would require more rework, and the sweet spot would move to the left, but probably to the 25 to 30 percent region rather than to the 10 to 15 percent region. On the other hand, the sweet spot for a high-assurance 10 KSLOC system would move to the right.

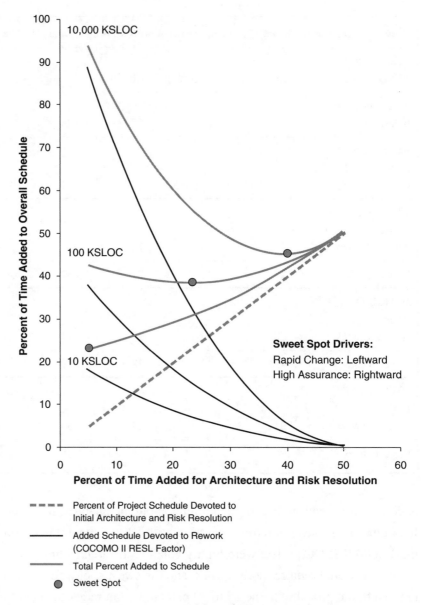

Sweet Spot Drivers:
Rapid Change: Leftward
High Assurance: Rightward

- - - - - Percent of Project Schedule Devoted to
         Initial Architecture and Risk Resolution

———— Added Schedule Devoted to Rework
         (COCOMO II RESL Factor)

———— Total Percent Added to Schedule

●   Sweet Spot

Figure E-4   How Much Architecting Is Enough?

This analysis is also a special case of balancing risk exposures, in which the fixed percentages of architecting investment and added rework effort in the COCOMO II model are sizes of losses that are assumed to occur with probability 1.0. Various other factors can affect the probability (and size) of loss associated with the RESL factor, such as staff capabilities, tool support, and technology uncertainties.[11] These could also be taken into account in a more detailed analysis.

E3. Experiments and Studies of Agile and Plan-Driven Methods

The comparisons above are largely qualitative, primarily because the lightweight nature of agile methods excludes much gathering of project data. But, as with the cost-of-change data discussed earlier, there is some relevant data, and it is often useful in determining under which project conditions one should use agile or plan-driven methods and what kind of results one should expect. In this section we summarize the additional empirical data we have identified on the overall size distribution of projects and the measurable effects of process improvement programs, TSP, agile methods, and pair programming.

Overall Distribution of Project Size

If agile methods are better for small projects and plan-driven methods are better for large projects, how many of each size project are there? As shown in Table E-2, the results vary by application sector. Financial-sector companies can have 65 percent small (< 10 people) projects while large aerospace companies have only around 10 percent, largely because the cost of government contracting for small projects is prohibitive. The COCOMO database figures between the 1970s and 1990s show a trend toward larger projects, most likely because they are easier to do with 1990s software technology, but partly because more of the data came from large companies.

Table E-2 Size Distribution by Application Sector

Sector/Database	% Small (< 10 people)	% Medium (11–50)	% Large (>50)
Finance	65	25	10
Auto sales	60	35	5
Telecom	40	40	20
Aerospace	10	50	40
COCOMO DB 1970s	62	33	5
COCOMO DB 1990s	41	47	12

The first three rows of Table E-2 were obtained from function point sizing expert David Garmus by Jim Highsmith, who used the data to emphasize the point that the agile methods' home ground in the small-projects area is where most projects fall.[12] From another perspective, the 65 percent small projects account for only 15 percent of the total staff size or amount of work being done, and most of the work is being done on the 10 percent large projects. This is even true in finance. Using average project sizes of 5 people (small), 25 people (medium), and 125 people (large), the corresponding percentages of total staff effort for financial projects are 15 percent small, 28 percent medium, and 57 percent large. Both perspectives are important to consider in organizational planning.

Process Improvement

The COCOMO II model includes a parameter (PMAT) for SW-CMM process maturity. This parameter was calibrated to the 161-project COCOMO II database, along with the 22 other parameters in the model.

The calibration indicated that the PMAT parameter was statistically significant, and that the effort saved per organizational maturity level ranged from 4 percent per level for small (10 KSLOC) applications to 10 percent per level for large (1,000 KSLOC) applications.

COCOMO II has separate parameters for other productivity improvement strategies involving such factors as personnel, tools, and reuse improvements. If an organization focuses on just process improvements, its payoff will be in the 4 to 10 percent per maturity level range. But the payoffs can be considerably higher for organizations combining process improvement with other productivity initiatives.

Several such examples were reported in Software Engineering Institute's "The 2001 High Maturity Workshop."[13] Boeing, Lockheed Martin, and Telos reported effort reduction levels of 60 to 82 percent and defect reduction levels of 69 to 87 percent, across three to four maturity levels and time spans of seven to ten years. These results reflected not just process improvement, but also improvements in tool support and reuse efficiency. In another example, Motorola's combined initiative was able to reduce project effort by 50 percent while going from SW-CMM Level 1 to Level 3.[14] Another large IT organization study[15] had a 67 percent decrease in defect rate in going from SW-CMM Level 1 to Level 2, and a 48 percent reduction in going from Level 2 to Level 3. However, the organization's productivity rate in SLOC/person-month decreased as well. These results are summarized with the other factors in Table E-3.

Team Software Process and Agile Methods

Table E-4 provides a comparative summary of reported data observed on the effects of TSP and agile methods on complete projects.

	Effects of SW-CMM Level on			Level	Baseline for
Study	Effort	Schedule	Defect Rate	Change	Comparison
COCOMO II, Small[10]	−17%			1–5	Regression analysis, 161 projects
COCOMO II, Large[10]	−48%			1–5	Regression analysis, 161 projects
Boeing[12]	−82%			2–5[†]	1991 vs.1999
Lockheed Martin[12]	−72%		−87%	3–5[†]	1992 vs. 1999
Telos[12]	−60%		−69%	1–4[†]	1990 vs. 2000
Motorola[13]	−50%			1–3[†]	Previous projects
Harter 2000[14]	Higher		−83%	1–3[†]	Previous projects

Table E-3 SW-CMM Process Improvement Results

X[†]: Includes effects of other initiatives (tools, reuse, etc.)

The main thing we notice about the observational data on TSP and agile methods is that everything that is reported succeeds spectacularly well. This could happen for a number of reasons:

- TSP and agile methods are indeed silver bullets and always succeed spectacularly well.
- People tend to report success more than they do failures.
- The pioneer projects are being done by high-capability early adopters of new methods.
- The pioneer projects are experiencing some Hawthorne effects of performing extra well while being in the spotlight.
- The projects are being compared to particularly poorly performing past projects.

Table E-4 Development Method Results					
	Effects of Practice on				
Study	**Effort**	**Schedule**	**Defect Rate**	**Satisfaction**	**Baseline for Comparison**
Team Software Process					
Webb 1999[16], 2000[17]	−55%		−50%	High	Previous projects
Vu 2000[18]			−89%	High	Previous projects
Pavlik 2002[19]	−42%		−90%		
Ciurczak 2002[20]		−37%			
Musson 2002[21], development	−28%		−95%	High	Previous project extrapolation
Musson 2002, lifetime	−62%			High	Previous project extrapolation
Agile Methods					
Stapleton 1997[22], DSDM	−74%			High	Non-DSDM module, same project
Maurer 2002[23], XP	−40%			High	Non-XP projects
Intelliware 2002[24], XP	−50–80%			High	Industry averages
Bowers 2002[25], XP	−69%		−61%	High	Previous waterfall project
Bowers 2002, XP	−38%		−61%	High	Previous OO project
Hodgetts 2003[26], XP	−41%		−10%	High	Version 3 vs. Version 2
Reifer 2002[27]	−13–19%	−25–50%	0%	High	Corporate baselines

In some cases, there is enough detail to identify major causes. For example, the "traditional project" compared to TSP in Musson's research had particularly poor performance in that it spent 66 percent of its development effort in integration and test and 49 percent of its lifetime effort in corrective maintenance. The standard percentages are 40 percent for integration and test (the 40-20-40 rule) and 15 percent for lifetime corrective maintenance. Certainly, though, the high improvement numbers make it worth exploring whether your organization might realize similar benefits.

The explanation for the success, however, is most likely a mixture of all five reasons. In the end, there is simply not enough empirical data yet to determine which reasons are dominant, or to predict what will happen when more mainstream organizations adopt TSP or agile methods.

The Reifer survey data is probably the most representative of mainstream software development, as it covers a number of organizations trying to assess under what conditions to adopt agile methods, particularly XP. Projects surveyed were almost all small (< 10 people), stable, in-house Web/client-server applications performed by young, experienced, motivated performers to assess the ability of agile methods to reduce the time to market. Most of the XP practices were strongly endorsed. On the other hand, having a full-time collocated customer and limiting people to 40 hours a week were found to be good aspirations but mostly unachievable in practice. Table E-5 summarizes the results.

Pair Programming
Table E-6 shows the effects of using pair programming (PP) obtained by experiments on the programming and development of small modules. The three experiments at the bottom of Table E-6 show relatively little improvement due to PP. This reflects the need for a pair-jelling

Industry	Number of Projects	Budget Performance[*]	Schedule Achievement[*]	Product Quality[†]
Aerospace	1	Better than average	Better than average	Below par
Computer	3	Average	Better than average	No data
Consultants	2	Average	Average	No data
E-business	15	Better than average	Better than average	Above par
Researchers	1	Average	Average	No data
Scientific	0	No data	No data	No data
Software	4	Average	Average	Par
Telecom	5	Better than average	Better than average	Par
Totals / (+, Average, −)	31	(3, 4, 0)	(4, 3, 0)	(1, 2, 1)

Table E-5 XP/Agile Method Scorecard (Reifer 2002)

[*]—"Average" represents what is normal performance for similar projects (using existing metrics)
[†]—"Par" represents nominal quality rating for their projects (using existing metrics)

phase of at least 10 hours before pairs become fully effective. This is a caution both for interpreting the results of PP experiments and for estimating PP productivity or velocity on projects with high personnel turnover.

The results in the Baheti study show that distributed PP can be done without significant losses in productivity, but again with a caution that it requires careful preparation and jelling. As many people expect PP to be awkward and unnerving, probably the most surprising outcome is the strong programmer preference for continuing to use PP once they have tried it.

For well-jelled, stable teams, PP appears about equivalent to inspections in adding about 10 to 15 percent to effort and eliminating about 60 percent of the defects.[28, 29] But PP's 45 percent reduction in schedule is extremely valuable whenever software is on the critical path in getting products to market.

Table E-6 Pair Programming Results						
	Effects of Practice on					
Study	**Effort**	**Schedule**	**Defect Rate**	**Satisfaction**	**Baseline for Comparison**	**Length (Hrs.)**
Pair Programming						
Nosek 1998[30]	+43%	−29%		High	Experiment vs. non-pairs	0.75
Williams 2000[31]	+15%	−43%	−60%	High	Experiment vs. non-pairs	>10
Baheti 2002[32]	+2%	−49%			Experiment: collocated	12–16
Baheti 2002	+14%	−43%			Experiment: distributed	12–16
Ciolkowski 2002[33]	+9%	−46%		High	Experiment vs. non-pairs	14
Nawrocki 2001[34]	+82%	−9%			Experiment vs. non-pairs	1–4
Rostaher 2002[35]	+98%	−1%		High	Experiment: mixed PP-test	6
Arisholm 2002[36]	+96%	−2%	−30%		Experiment vs. non-pairs	1

In addition to the impact on schedule and defect reduction, PP provides an interproject communication function that is nearly essential for agile methods and highly valuable for plan-driven methods. PP results in a level of shared, detailed knowledge of the software across the development team that is difficult to achieve in other ways.

Without PP and without documentation, agile methods are essentially dependent on collocation and standup meetings to communicate this tacit knowledge and to serve as insurance against personnel turnover. This insurance is equally valuable for plan-driven methods. In regions with a high demand-to-supply ratio for programmers (e.g., Silicon Valley a few years ago, India now), personnel turnover is a project's number one risk. PP's teambuilding and detailed knowledge sharing can strongly reduce both components of this risk—the probability of people leaving the team and the impact on the knowledge base when people do leave. The personnel turnover will have some impact on project productivity or velocity due to rejelling effects, but the impact will be considerably less than otherwise.

Hybrid Agile/Plan-Driven Methods

A hybrid agile/plan-driven method called Code Science or AgilePlus has been used successfully on 14 projects between 10 and 409 KSLOC in size over the years 1998 to 2002. It uses most of the XP practices, except for the 40-hour week, and only partially uses pair programming. It combines these practices with such plan-driven methods as a componentized architecture, risk-based situation audits, business process analyses, and on-demand document generation. The median and mean productivity rates over the 14 projects are 1,657 and 1,778 SLOC per person-month, as compared to a range of 600 to 900 SLOC per person-month for traditional plan-driven projects at the same organization.[37, 38]

Notes

Chapter One

1. Paulk, M.C., et al. February 1993. *Capability Maturity Model for Software, Version 1.1.* CMU/SEI-93-TR-24, ADA263403. Pittsburgh: Software Engineering Institute, Carnegie-Mellon University.

2. Crosby, P.B. 1979. *Quality Is Free.* New York: McGraw-Hill.

3. Deming, W.E. 1986. *Out of the Crisis.* Cambridge, MA: MIT Center for Advanced Engineering.

4. Juran, J.M. 1988. *Juran on Planning for Quality.* New York: MacMillan.

5. Humphrey, W. 1989. *Managing the Software Process.* Reading, MA: Addison-Wesley.

6. CMMI Development Team. 2001. *CMMI-SE/SW/IPPD, V1.1: Capability Maturity Model Integrated for Systems Engineering, Software Engineering and Integrated Product and Process Development, Version 1.1: continuous representation.* Pittsburgh: Software Engineering Institute, Carnegie-Mellon University; p. 688.

7. Ahern, D.M., A. Clouse, R. Turner. 2001. *CMMI Distilled: A Practical Introduction to Integrated Process Improvement.* Boston: Addison-Wesley.

8. Agile Alliance. 2001. "Manifesto for Agile Software Development." http://www.agilealliance.org.

9. Paulk, M. October 2002. "Agile Methodologies and Process Discipline," *CrossTalk.* Hill Air Force Base, Utah: U.S. Air Force Software Technology Support Center; pp. 15–18.

10. Sheard, S. July 2003. "The Life Cycle of a Silver Bullet," *CrossTalk.* Hill Air Force Base, Utah: U.S. Air Force Software Technology Support Center.

11. Hock, D. 1999. *Birth of the Chaordic Age.* San Francisco: Berrett-Koehler Publishers.

12. Cockburn, A. 2002. "Agile Software Development Joins the 'Would-Be Crowd,'" *Cutter IT Journal;* Vol. 15, No. 1, pp. 6–12.

13. CeBASE e-Workshop summary. 2002. www.cebase.org.

14. Williams, L., and R. Kessler. 2002. *Pair Programming Illuminated.* Boston: Addison-Wesley.

15. Beck, K. 1999. *Extreme Programming Explained.* Reading, MA: Addison-Wesley.

16. Highsmith, J. 2002. *Agile Software Development Ecosystems.* Boston: Addison-Wesley.

17. *Second XP Universe and First Agile Universe Conference 2002 Proceedings.* August 2002. Don Wells and Laurie Williams, eds. LNCS 2418, Lecture Notes in Computer Science Series, G. Goos, et al., eds. Heidelberg/New York: Springer.

18. Cusumano, M., and D. Yoffie. 2000. *Competing on Internet Time.* Carmichael, CA: Touchstone Books.

19. Britcher, R.N. 1999. *The Limits of Software.* Reading, MA: Addison-Wesley.

20. Kruchten, P. 2002. Presentation to the Iterative, Adaptive, and Agile Processes Workshop at ICSE 2002.

Chapter Two

1. Beck, K. 1999. *Extreme Programming Explained.* Boston: Addison-Wesley; p. 157.

2. Constantine, L. June 2001. "Methodological Agility," *Software Development;* pp. 67–69.

3. McBreen, P. 2003. *Questioning Extreme Programmin*g. Boston: Addison-Wesley; p. 100.

4. Highsmith, J. 2002. *Agile Software Development Ecosystems.* Boston: Addison-Wesley.

5. Highsmith, J. 2002. *Agile Software Development Ecosystems.* Boston: Addison-Wesley.

6. Cockburn, A., and J. Highsmith. November 2001. "Agile Software Development: The People Factor," *Computer;* pp. 131–133.

7. Sliwa, C. March 18, 2002. "Users Warm Up to Agile Programming," *Computerworld;* p. 8.

8. Results of the 3rd e-Workshop on agile development processes. 2002. www.cebase.org.

9. Boehm, B. May 1988. "A Spiral Model for Software Development and Enhancement," *Computer;* Vol. 21, pp. 61–72.

10. McBreen, P. 2003. *Questioning Extreme Programming.* Boston: Addison-Wesley.

11. Gause, D., and G. Weinberg. 1989. *Exploring Requirements: Quality before Design.* New York: Dorset House.

12. Carnegie Mellon University, Software Engineering Institute, 1995. *The Capability Maturity Model.* Reading, MA: Addison-Wesley.

13. Boehm, B., and W. Hansen. May 2001. "The Spiral Model as a Tool for Evolutionary Acquisition," *CrossTalk*. Hill Air Force Base, Utah: U.S. Air Force Software Technology Support Center; Vol. 14, pp. 4–11.

14. Beck, K. 1999. *Extreme Programming Explained*. Reading, MA: Addison-Wesley; p. 103.

15. Li, W., and M. Alshayeb. 2001. "An Empirical Study of Extreme Programming Process," *Proceedings, 17th Intl. COCOMO/Software Cost Modeling Forum*. USC-CSE.

16. Reifer, D. "How to Get the Most out of Extreme Programming/Agile Methods," *Proceedings, XP/Agile Universe 2002*. Springer; pp. 185–196.

17. Boehm, B. March 2000. "Unifying Software Engineering and Systems Engineering," *Computer;* pp. 114–116.

18. Van Cauwenberghe, P. 2003. "Refactoring or Up-Front Design?" in Marchesi, M. et al., ed. *Extreme Programming Perspectives*. Boston: Addison-Wesley; pp. 191–200.

19. Lim, W. 1998. *Managing Software Reuse*. Englewood Cliffs, NJ: Prentice-Hall.

20. Malan, R., and K. Wentzel. April 1993. "Economics of Reuse Revisited," HP Labs Technical Report HPL-93-31.

21. Poulin, J. 1997. *Measuring Software Reuse*. Reading, MA: Addison-Wesley.

22. Reifer, D. 1997. *Practical Software Reuse*. New York: John Wiley and Sons.

23. Lim, W. 1998. *Managing Software Reuse*. Englewood Cliffs, NJ: Prentice-Hall.

24. Beck, K. 2003. *Test Driven Development—by Example*. Boston: Addison-Wesley.

25. McBreen, P. 2003. *Questioning Extreme Programming*. Boston: Addison-Wesley.

26. Van Duersen, A. November 2001. "Customer Involvement in Extreme Programming," *ACM Software Engineering Notes;* pp. 70–73.

27. Britcher, R.N. 1999. *The Limits of Software*. Reading, MA: Addison-Wesley.

28. Highsmith, J., and A. Cockburn. September 2001. "Agile Software Development: The Business of Innovation," *Computer;* pp. 120–122.

29. Constantine, L. June 2001. "Methodological Agility," *Software Development;* pp. 67–69.

30. Cockburn, A. 2002. *Agile Software Development*. Boston: Addison-Wesley

31. Highsmith, J. 2002. *Agile Software Development Ecosystems*. Boston: Addison-Wesley.

32. Cockburn, A. 2002. *Agile Software Development*. Boston: Addison-Wesley.

33. Paulk, M. October 2002. "Agile Methodologies and Process Discipline," *CrossTalk*. Hill Air Force Base, Utah: U.S. Air Force Software Technology Support Center; Vol. 15, No. 10, pp. 15–18.

34. Peters, T. 1991. *Thriving on Chaos*. New York: HarperCollins.

Chapter Three

1. Humphrey, W. 2000. *Introduction to Team Software Process*. Boston: Addison-Wesley, p. 256.

2. Adapted from *Disciplined Software Development*. 1999. Hill Air Force Base, Utah: U.S. Air Force Software Technology Support Center. http://stsc. hill.af.mil.

3. Humphrey, W. 2000. *Introduction to Team Software Process*. Boston: Addison-Wesley, p. 353.

Chapter Four

1. Elssamadisy, A., and G. Schalliol. 2002. "Recognizing and Responding to 'Bad Smells' in Extreme Programming," *Proceedings, ICSE 2002;* pp. 617–622.

2. Fowler, M. 1999. *Refactoring*. Reading, MA: Addison-Wesley; Chapter 3.

3. Boehm, B., and V. Basili. January 2001. "Software Defect Reduction Top 10 List," *IEEE Computer;* Vol. 34, No. 1, pp. 135–137.

4. Highsmith, J. 2002. *Agile Software Development Ecosystems*. Boston: Addison-Wesley.

5. Royce, W.E. 1998. *Software Project Management: A Unified Framework*. Reading, MA: Addison-Wesley; pp. 299–362.

6. Royce, W.E. 1998. *Software Project Management: A Unified Framework*. Reading, MA: Addison-Wesley; p. 345.

7. Cockburn, A. 2002. *Agile Software Development*. Boston: Addison-Wesley.

Chapter Five

1. Boehm, B. 1981. *Software Engineering Economics*. Englewood Cliffs, NJ: Prentice-Hall PTR; Chapter 20.

2. Boehm, B., and W. Hansen. May 2001. "The Spiral Model as a Tool for Evolutionary Acquisition," *CrossTalk*. Hill Air Force Base, Utah: U.S. Air Force Software Technology Support Center; Vol. 14, pp. 4–11.

3. B. Boehm. July 1996. "Anchoring the Software Process," *IEEE Software;* pp. 73–82.

4. Jacobson, I., G. Booch, and J. Rumbaugh. 1999. *The Unified Software Development Process*. Reading, MA: Addison-Wesley.

5. Boehm, B., and D. Port. December 2001. "Balancing Discipline and Flexibility with the Spiral Model and MBASE," *CrossTalk*. Hill Air Force Base, Utah: U.S. Air Force Software Technology Support Center; Vol. 11, pp. 23–28.

6. Anthes, G. January 27, 2003. "Agents of Change," *Computerworld;* pp. 26–27.

7. Elssamadisy, A., and G. Schalliol. 2002. "Recognizing and Responding to 'Bad Smells' in Extreme Programming," *Proceedings, ICSE 2002;* pp. 617–622.

8. Thorp, J. 1998. *The Information Paradox*. McGraw-Hill.

9. Parnas, D. March 1979. "Designing Software for Ease of Extension and Contraction," *IEEE Transactions on Software Engineering;* pp. 128–137.

10. Boehm, B., and W. Hansen. May 2001. "The Spiral Model as a Tool for Evolutionary Acquisition," *CrossTalk*. Hill Air Force Base, Utah: U.S. Air Force Software Technology Support Center; Vol. 14, pp. 4–11.

11. Schwaber, K., and M. Beedle. 2002. *Agile Software Development with Scrum*. Upper Saddle River, NJ: Prentice-Hall; p. 20.

12. Basili, V., and B. Boehm. May 2001. "COTS-Based Systems Top 10 List," *IEEE Computer*.

13. Boehm, B., and W. Hansen. May 2001. "The Spiral Model as a Tool for Evolutionary Acquisition," *CrossTalk*. Hill Air Force Base, Utah: U.S. Air Force Software Technology Support Center; Vol. 14, pp. 4–11.

14. Manzo, J. October 2002. "Odyssey and Other Code Science Success Stories," *CrossTalk*. Hill Air Force Base, Utah: U.S. Air Force Software Technology Support Center; pp. 19–21, 30.

15. Manzo, J. March 2003. "Agile Development Methods, the Myths, and the Reality: A User Perspective," *Proceedings, USC-CSE Agile Methods Workshop;* http://sunset.usc.edu/events/past.

Chapter Six

1. Brooks, F. 1986. "No Silver Bullet," *Information Processing 1986, Proceedings of the IFIP Tenth World Computing Conference,* H.-J. Kugler, ed. Amsterdam: Elsevier Science B.V.; pp. 1069–1076.

2. Weinberg, G. 1971. *The Psychology of Computer Programming*. New York: Van Nostrand-Reinhold.

3. Ehn, P. (ed.). March 1990. *Work-Oriented Design of Computer Artifacts*. Mahwah, NJ: Lawrence Earlbaum Associates.

4. DeMarco, T., and T. Lister. 1999. *Peopleware: Productive Projects and Teams*. New York: Dorset House.

5. Curtis, B., H. Krasner, and N. Iscoe. November 1988. "A Field Study of the Software Design Process for Large Systems," *Communications of the ACM;* 31 (11), pp. 1268–1287.

6. Curtis, B., et al. 2001. *People Capability Maturity Model.* Boston: Addison-Wesley.

7. Grant, E., and H. Sackman. September 1966. "An Exploratory Investigation of Programmer Performance under On-Line and Off-Line Conditions," Report SP-2581. System Development Corp.

8. Boehm, B. 1981. *Software Engineering Economics.* Upper Saddle River, NJ: Prentice-Hall.

9. Boehm, B., et al. 2000. *Software Cost Estimation with COCOMO II.* Upper Saddle River, NJ: Prentice-Hall.

10. Dijkstra, E. 1979. Panel discussion, Fourth International Conference on Software Engineering, Munich.

11. Carnegie Mellon University, Software Engineering Institute, 1995. *The Capability Maturity Model.* Reading, MA: Addison-Wesley.

12. Tucker, A. September-October 2002. "On the Balance between Theory and Practice," *IEEE Software*.

13. Highsmith, J. 2002. *Agile Software Development Ecosystems.* Boston: Addison-Wesley.

14. Cockburn, A. 2002. *Agile Software Development.* Boston: Addison-Wesley.

15. Humphrey, W. 1997. *Managing Technical People.* Reading, MA: Addison-Wesley.

16. Humphrey, W. 1995. *A Discipline of Programming.* Reading, MA: Addison-Wesley.

17. Humphrey, W. 1997. *Introduction to the Personal Software Process.* Reading, MA: Addison-Wesley.

18. Curtis, B., B. Hefley, and S. Miller. 2001. *The People Capability Maturity Model.* Boston: Addison Wesley

19. Boehm, B. March 2003. "Value-Based Software Engineering," *ACM Software Engineering Notes.*

20. McGarry, J., and R. Charette. 2003. "Systemic Analysis of Assessment Results from DoD Software-Intensive System Acquisitions," Tri-Service Assessment Initiative Report, Office of the Under Secretary of Defense (Acquisition, Technology, Logistics).

21. Collins, J. 2001. *Good to Great.* New York: HarperCollins.

22. Boehm, B. March 2003. "Value-Based Software Engineering," *ACM Software Engineering Notes.*

23. Kaplan, R., D. Norton. 1996. *The Balanced Scorecard: Translating Strategy into Action.* Boston: Harvard Business School Press.

24. Karten, N., and G. Weinberg. January 1994. *Expectations Management.* New York: Dorset House.

25. Karten, N. May 2002. *Communication Gaps and How to Close Them.* New York: Dorset House.

Appendix C

1. Paulk, M., et al. August 1991. *Capability Maturity Model for Software.* CMU/SEI-91-TR-24, DTIC Number ADA240603. Pittsburgh: Software Engineering Institute, Carnegie-Mellon University.

2. Paulk, M., et al. February 1993. *The Capability Maturity Model for Software V1.1.* CMU/SEI-93-TR-24, DTIC Number ADA263403. Pittsburgh: Software Engineering Institute, Carnegie-Mellon University.

3. Carnegie Mellon University, Software Engineering Institute, 1995. *The Capability Maturity Model.* Reading, MA: Addison-Wesley.

4. CMMI Development Team. 2002. *Capability Maturity Model Integration V1.1.* CMU/SEI-2002-TR-011. Pittsburgh: Software Engineering Institute, Carnegie-Mellon University.

5. Ahern, D., A. Clouse, and R. Turner. 2001. *CMMI Distilled: A Practical Introduction to Integrated Process Improvement (2nd Ed. 2003).* Boston: Addison-Wesley.

6. Chrissis, M., M. Konrad, and S. Shrum. 2003. *CMMI: Guidelines for Process Integration and Product Improvement.* Boston: Addison-Wesley.

7. In January 1993, an international working group (WG 10) was formed as part of subcommittee 7 (SC7) of the ISO/IEC Joint Technical Committee 1 (JTC1) to create a standard for software process assessment. Piloting of working drafts was accomplished through a project called SPICE (Software Process Improvement and Capability Determination). The combined effort of WG 10 and the SPICE project resulted in the development of ISO/IEC 15504.

Appendix D

1. Boehm, B. July 1996. "Anchoring the Software Process," *IEEE Software;* pp. 73–82.

2. Royce, W.E. 1998. *Software Project Management: A Unified Framework.* Reading, MA: Addison-Wesley.

3. Kruchten, P. 1999. *The Rational Unified Process (2nd Ed. 2001).* Reading, MA: Addison-Wesley.

4. Jacobson, I., G. Booch, and J. Rumbaugh. 1999. *The Unified Software Development Process.* Reading, MA: Addison-Wesley.

5. Boehm, B., A. Egyed, J. Kwan, D. Port, A. Shah, and R. Madachy. July 1998. "Using the Win-Win Spiral Model: A Case Study," *Computer;* pp. 33–44.

6. USC-CSE. "MBASE Guidelines" and "MBASE Electronic Process Guide." http://sunset.usc.edu/research/MBASE.

7. Boehm, B., D. Port, A. Jain, and V. Basili. May 2002. "Achieving CMMI Level 5 Improvements with MBASE and the CeBASE Method," *CrossTalk.* Hill Air Force Base, Utah: U.S. Air Force Software Technology Support Center; pp. 9–16.

8. Marenzano, J. 1995. "System Architecture Validation Review Findings," in D. Garlan, ed., *ICSE Architecture Workshop Proceedings.* Pittsburgh: Carnegie-Mellon University.

9. Defense Science Board. November 2000. "Report of the Defense Science Board Task Force on Defense Software," Office of the Under Secretary of Defense (Acquisition, Technology, Logistics).

10. Boehm, B. July 1996. "Anchoring the Software Process," *IEEE Software;* pp. 73–82.

11. Thorp, J., and DMR. 1998. *The Information Paradox.* New York: McGraw-Hill.

12. Boehm, B., D. Port, L. Huang, and A.W. Brown. January 2002. "Using the Spiral Model and MBASE to Generate New Acquisition Process Models: SAIV, CAIV, and SCQAIV," *CrossTalk.* Hill Air Force Base, Utah: U.S. Air Force Software Technology Support Center; pp. 20–25.

13. Yourdon, E. 1999. *Death March: The Complete Software Developer's Guide to Surviving "Mission Impossible" Projects.* Upper Saddle River, NJ: Prentice-Hall PTR.

14. Boehm, B., M. Abi-Antoun, J. Kwan, A. Lynch, and D. Port. June 1999. "Requirements Engineering, Expectations Management, and the Two Cultures," *Proceedings, 1999 International Conference on Requirements Engineering.*

15. Boehm, B., P. Grünbacher, P., and R. Briggs. May/June 2001. "Developing Groupware for Requirements Negotiation: Lessons Learned," *IEEE Software;* Vol. 18, No. 3.

16. Boehm, B., C. Abts, A.W. Brown, S. Chulani, B. Clark, E. Horowitz, R. Madachy, D. Reifer, and B. Steece. 2000. *Software Cost Estimation with COCOMO II.* Englewood Cliffs, NJ: Prentice-Hall.

17. Parnas, D. March 1979. "Designing Software for Ease of Extension and Contraction," *IEEE Trans. Software Engineering;* pp. 128–137.

Appendix E

1. Beck, K. 1999. *Extreme Programming Explained.* Reading, MA: Addison-Wesley.
2. Erdogmus, H., and J. Favaro. 2003. "Keep Your Options Open: Extreme Programming and the Economics of Flexibility," in Marchesi, M. et al., ed., *Extreme Programming Perspectives.* Boston: Addison-Wesley; pp. 503–552.
3. Boehm, B. 1981. *Software Engineering Economics.* Englewood Cliffs, NJ: Prentice-Hall PTR.
4. Shull, et al. June 2002. "What We Have Learned about Fighting Defects," *Proceedings, Metrics 2002.* IEEE; pp. 249–258.
5. McGibbon, T. 1996. "Software Reliability Data Summary," Data Analysis Center for Software Technical Report.
6. Li, W., and M. Alshayeb. 2002. "An Empirical Study of Extreme Programming Process," *Proceedings 17th Intl. COCOMO/Software Cost Modeling Forum.* USC-CSE.
7. Reifer, D. 2002. "How to Get the Most Out of Extreme Programming/Agile Methods," *Proceedings, XP/Agile Universe 2002.* New York: Springer; pp. 185–196.
8. B. Boehm, C. Abts, A.W. Brown, S. Chulani, B. Clark, E. Horowitz, R. Madachy,D. Reifer, and B. Steece. 2000. *Software Cost Estimation with COCOMO II.* Englewood Cliffs, NJ: Prentice-Hall.
9. Rechtin, E. 1991. *Systems Architecting.* Englewood Cliffs, NJ: Prentice-Hall.
10. McBreen, P. 2003. *Questioning Extreme Programming.* Boston: Addison-Wesley.
11. B. Boehm, C. Abts, A.W. Brown, S. Chulani, B. Clark, E. Horowitz, R. Madachy, D. Reifer, and B. Steece. 2000. *Software Cost Estimation with COCOMO II.* Englewood Cliffs, NJ: Prentice-Hall.
12. Highsmith, J. 2002. *Agile Software Development Ecosystems.* Boston: Addison-Wesley.
13. Paulk, M., and M. Chrissis. January 2002. *The 2001 High Maturity Workshop.* CMU-SEI-2-1-SR-014. Pittsburgh: Software Engineering Institute, Carnegie-Mellon University.
14. Diaz, M., and J. Sligo. May 1997. "How Software Process Improvement Helped Motorola," *Software* 14(5); pp. 75–81.

15. Harter, D., M. Krishnan, and S. Slaughter. April 2000. "Effects of Process Maturity on Quality, Cycle Time, and Effort in Software Product Development," *Management Science;* pp. 451–466.

16. Webb, D., and W. Humphrey. February 1999. "Using TSP on the Task View Project," *CrossTalk.* Hill Air Force Base, Utah: U.S. Air Force Software Technology Support Center; pp. 3–10.

17. Webb, D. June 2000. "Managing Risk with TSP," *CrossTalk.* Hill Air Force Base, Utah: U.S. Air Force Software Technology Support Center.

18. Vu, J. March 2000. "Process Improvement in the Boeing Company," *Proceedings, Software Engineering Process Group 2000.* Pittsburgh: Software Engineering Institute.

19. Pavlik, R., and C. Riall. February 2002. "Integrating PSP, TSP, and Six Sigma at Honeywell," *Proceedings, Software Engineering Process Group 2002.* Pittsburgh: Software Engineering Institute.

20. Ciurczak, J. February 2002. "The Quiet Quality Revolution at EBS Dealing Resources," *Proceedings, Software Engineering Process Group 2002.* Pittsburgh: Software Engineering Institute.

21. Musson, R. September 2002. "How the TSP Impacts the Top Line," *CrossTalk,* Hill Air Force Base, Utah: U.S. Air Force Software Technology Support Center; pp. 9–11.

22. Stapleton, J. 1997. *Dynamic Systems Development Method.* Reading, MA: Addison-Wesley.

23. Maurer, R., and S. Martel. April 8, 2002. "Agile Software Development: An Industrial Case Study," CeBASE Agile Methods e-Workshop No. 1. http://fc-md.umd.edu/projects/Agile/Maurer.htm.

24. Intelliware Development, Inc. October 25, 2002. "XP Metrics" presentation.

25. Bowers, J., et al. 2002. "Tailoring XP for Large-System Mission-Critical Software Development," *Proceedings, XP/Agile Universe 2002.* New York: Springer.

26. Hodgetts, P., and D. Philips. 2003. "Extreme Adoption Experiences of a B2B Startup," in Marchesi, et al., ed., *Extreme Programming Perspectives.* Boston: Addison-Wesley; pp. 355–362.

27. Reifer, D. 2002. "How to Get the Most Out of Extreme Programming/Agile Methods," *Proceedings, XP/Agile Universe 2002.* New York: Springer; pp. 185–196.

28. Boehm, B., and V. Basili. January 2001. "Software Defect Reduction Top 10 List," *IEEE Computer.*

29. Shull, et al. June 2002. "What We Have Learned about Fighting Defects," *Proceedings, Metrics 2002*. IEEE; pp. 249–258.

30. Nosek, J. March 1998. "The Case for Collaborative Programming," *Communications of the ACM;* pp. 105–108.

31. Williams, L., R. Kessler, W. Cunningham, and R. Jeffries. August 2000. "Strengthening the Case for Pair Programming," *Software;* pp. 19–25.

32. Baheti, P., E. Gehringer, and D. Stotts. 2002. "Exploring the Efficacy of Distributed Pair Programming," *Proceedings, XP/Agile Universe 2002*. New York: Springer; pp. 208–220.

33. Ciolkowski, M., and M. Schlemmer. October 2002. "Studying the Effect of Pair Programming," *Proceedings, ISERN 2002*.

34. Nawrocki, J., and Wojciechowski. 2001. "Experimental Evaluation of Pair Programming," *Proceedings, ESCOM 2001;* pp. 269–276.

35. Rostaher, M., and M. Hericko. 2002. "Tracking Test-First Pair Programming—An Experiment," *Proceedings, XP/Agile Universe 2002*. New York: Springer; pp. 174–184.

36. Arisholm, E. October 2002. "Design of a Controlled Experiment on Pair Programming," *Proceedings, ISERN 2002*.

37. Manzo, J. October 2002. "Odyssey and Other Code Science Success Stories," *CrossTalk,* Hill Air Force Base, Utah: U.S. Air Force Software Technology Support Center; pp. 19–21, 30.

38. Manzo, J. March 2003. "Agile Development Methods, the Myths, and the Reality: A User Perspective," *Proceedings, USC-CSE Agile Methods Workshop*. http://sunset.usc.edu/events/past.

References

Abrahamsson, P., O. Salo, J. Ronkainen, and J. Warsta. 2002. *Agile Software Development Methods*. Espoo, Finland: Technical Research Centre of Finland. VTT Publication 478. http://www.inf.vtt.fi/pdf/publications/2002/p478.pdf.

Agile Alliance. 2001. "Manifesto for Agile Software Development." http://www.agilealliance.org.

Ahern, D.M., A. Clouse, R. Turner. 2001. *CMMI Distilled: A Practical Introduction to Integrated Process Improvement (2nd Ed. 2003)*. Boston: Addison-Wesley.

Anthes, G. January 27, 2003. "Agents of Change," *Computerworld*; pp. 26–27.

Arisholm, E. October 2002. "Design of a Controlled Experiment on Pair Programming," *Proceedings, ISERN 2002*.

Baheti, P., E. Gehringer, and D. Stotts. 2002. "Exploring the Efficacy of Distributed Pair Programming," *Proceedings, XP/Agile Universe 2002*. Springer; pp. 208–220.

Basili, V., and B. Boehm. May 2001. "COTS-Based Systems Top 10 List," *IEEE Computer*.

Beck, K. 2003. *Test Driven Development—By Example*. Boston: Addison-Wesley.

Beck, K. 1999. *Extreme Programming Explained*. Reading, MA: Addison-Wesley.

Becker, S., and J. Whittaker. 1997. *Cleanroom Software Engineering Practices (4th Ed.)*. Hershey, PA: Idea Group Publishing Co.

Boehm, B. March 2003. "Value-Based Software Engineering," *ACM Software Engineering Notes*.

Boehm, B. March 2000. "Unifying Software Engineering and Systems Engineering," *Computer*; pp. 114–116.

Boehm, B. July 1996. "Anchoring the Software Process," *IEEE Software*; pp. 73–82.

Boehm, B. May 1988. "A Spiral Model for Software Development and Enhancement," *Computer*, Vol. 21; pp. 61–72.

Boehm, B. 1981. *Software Engineering Economics*. Prentice-Hall PTR; Chapter 20.

Boehm, B., and V. Basili. January 2001. "Software Defect Reduction Top 10 List," *IEEE Computer*.

Boehm, B., and W. Hansen. May 2001. "The Spiral Model as a Tool for Evolution-ary Acquisition," *CrossTalk*. Hill Air Force Base, Utah: U.S. Air Force Soft-ware Technology Support Center; Vol. 14; pp. 4–11.

Boehm, B., and D. Port. December 2001. "Balancing Discipline and Flexibility with the Spiral Model and MBASE," *CrossTalk*. Hill Air Force Base, Utah: U.S. Air Force Software Technology Support Center; Vol. 11; pp. 23–28.

Boehm, B., M. Abi-Antoun, J. Kwan, A. Lynch, and D. Port. June 1999. "Re-quirements Engineering, Expectations Management, and the Two Cultures," *Proceedings, 1999 International Conference on Requirements Engineering*.

Boehm, B., C. Abts, A.W. Brown, S. Chulani, B. Clark, E. Horowitz, R. Madachy, D. Reifer, and B. Steece. 2000. *Software Cost Estimation with COCOMO II*. Englewood Cliffs, NJ: Prentice-Hall.

Boehm, B., A. Egyed, J. Kwan, D. Port, A. Shah, and R. Madachy. July 1998. "Using the Win-Win Spiral Model: A Case Study," *Computer*; pp. 33–44.

Boehm, B., P. Grünbacher, P., and R. Briggs. May/June 2001. "Developing Group-ware for Requirements Negotiation: Lessons Learned," *IEEE Software*; Vol. 18, No. 3.

Boehm, B., D. Port, L. Huang, and A.W. Brown. January 2002. "Using the Spiral Model and MBASE to Generate New Acquisition Process Models: SAIV, CAIV, and SCQAIV," *CrossTalk*. Hill Air Force Base, Utah: U.S. Air Force Software Technology Support Center; pp. 20–25.

Boehm, B., D. Port, A. Jain, and V. Basili. May 2002. "Achieving CMMI Level 5 Improvements with MBASE and the CeBASE Method," *CrossTalk*. Hill Air Force Base, Utah: U.S. Air Force Software Technology Support Center; pp. 9–16.

Bowers, J., et al. 2002. "Tailoring XP for Large-System Mission-Critical Software Development," *Proceedings, XP/Agile Universe 2002*. New York: Springer.

Britcher, R.N. 1999. *The Limits of Software*. Reading, MA: Addison-Wesley.

Brooks, F. 1986. "No Silver Bullet," *Information Processing 1986, Proceedings of the IFIP Tenth World Computing Conference*, H.-J. Kugler, ed. Amsterdam: Elsevier Science B.V.; pp. 1069–1076.

Carnegie Mellon University, Software Engineering Institute, 1995. *The Capability Maturity Model*. Reading, MA: Addison-Wesley.

CeBASE e-Workshop summary. 2002. www.cebase.org.

Chrissis, M., M. Konrad, and S. Shrum. 2003. *CMMI: Guidelines for Process Inte-gration and Product Improvement*. Boston: Addison-Wesley.

Ciolkowski, M., and M. Schlemmer. October 2002. "Studying the Effect of Pair Programming," *Proceedings, ISERN 2002*.

Ciurczak, J. February 2002. "The Quiet Quality Revolution at EBS Dealing Resources," *Proceedings, SEPG 2002.* SEI.

CMMI Development Team. 2002. *Capability Maturity Model Integration V1.1.* CMU/SEI-2002-TR-011. Pittsburgh: Software Engineering Institute/Carnegie-Mellon University.

CMMI Development Team. 2001. *CMMI-SE/SW/IPPD, V1.1: Capability Maturity Model Integrated for Systems Engineering, Software Engineering and Integrated Product and Process Development, Version 1.1: Continuous Representation.* Pittsburgh: Software Engineering Institute/Carnegie-Mellon University; p. 688.

Coad, P., E. LeFebvre, and J. DeLuca. 2000. *Java Modeling in Color with UML.* Upper Saddle River, NJ: Prentice Hall.

The Coad Letter. www.togethercommunity.com.

Cockburn, A. 2002. *Agile Software Development.* Boston: Addison-Wesley.

Cockburn, A. 2002. "Agile Software Development Joins the 'Would-Be Crowd,'" *Cutter IT Journal*, Vol. 15, No. 1; pp. 6–12.

Cockburn, A. 2000. *Writing Effective Use Cases: The Crystal Collection for Software Professionals.* Boston: Addison-Wesley.

Cockburn, A., and J. Highsmith. November 2001. "Agile Software Development: The People Factor," *Computer*; pp. 131–133.

http://alistair.cockburn.us

Collins, J. 2001. *Good to Great.* New York: HarperCollins.

Constantine, L. June 2001. "Methodological Agility," *Software Development*; pp. 67–69. www.controlchaos.com

Crosby, P.B. 1979. *Quality Is Free.* New York: McGraw-Hill.

Curtis, B., H. Krasner, and N. Iscoe. November 1988. "A Field Study of the Software Design Process for Large Systems," *Communications of the ACM,* 31 (11); pp. 1268–1287.

Curtis, B., et al. 2001. *People Capability Maturity Model.* Boston: Addison-Wesley.

Cusumano, M., and D. Yoffie. 2000. *Competing on Internet Time.* Carmichael, CA: Touchstone Books.

Defense Science Board. November 2000. "Report of the Defense Science Board Task Force on Defense Software," Office of the Under Secretary of Defense (Acquisition, Technology, Logistics).

DeMarco, T., and T. Lister. 1999. *Peopleware: Productive Projects and Teams.* New York: Dorset House.

Deming, W. Edward. 1986. *Out of the Crisis.* Cambridge, MA: MIT Center for Advanced Engineering.

Diaz, M., and J. Sligo. May 1997. "How Software Process Improvement Helped Motorola," *Software,* 14(5); pp. 75–81.

Dijkstra, E. 1979. Panel discussion, Fourth International Conference on Software Engineering.

Disciplined Software Development. 1999. Hill Air Force Base, Utah: U.S. Air Force Software Technology Support Center. http://stsc.hill.af.mil.

DSDM Consortium. 1997. *Dynamic Systems Development Method, Version 3.* Ashford, England: DSDM Consortium.

Ehn, P. (ed.). March 1990. *Work-Oriented Design of Computer Artifacts.* Mahwah, NJ: Lawrence Earbaum Associates.

Elssamadisy, A., and G. Schalliol. 2002. "Recognizing and Responding to 'Bad Smells' in Extreme Programming," *Proceedings, ICSE 2002*; pp. 617–622.

Erdogmus, H., and J. Favaro. 2003. "Keep Your Options Open: Extreme Programming and the Economics of Flexibility," in Marchesi, et al., ed. *Extreme Programming Perspectives.* Boston: Addison-Wesley; pp. 503–552.

Fowler, M. 1999. *Refactoring.* Reading, MA: Addison-Wesley; Chapter 3.

Gause, D., and G. Weinberg. 1989. *Exploring Requirements: Quality before Design.* New York: Dorset House.

Grant, E., and H. Sackman. September 1966. "An Exploratory Investigation of Programmer Performance Under On-Line and Off-Line Conditions," Report SP-2581. System Development Corp.

Harter, D., M. Krishnan, and S. Slaughter. April 2000. "Effects of Process Maturity on Quality, Cycle Time, and Effort in Software Product Development," *Management Science*; pp. 451–466.

Highsmith, J. 2002. *Agile Software Development Ecosystems.* Boston: Addison-Wesley.

Highsmith, J. 2000. *Adaptive Software Development: A Collaborative Approach to Managing Complex Systems.* New York: Dorset House.

Highsmith, J., and A. Cockburn. September 2001. "Agile Software Development: The Business of Innovation," *Computer*; pp. 120–122.

Hock, D. 1999. *Birth of the Chaordic Age.* San Francisco: Berrett-Koehler Publishers.

Hodgetts, P., and D. Philips. 2003. "Extreme Adoption Experiences of a B2B Startup," in Marchesi, et al., ed., *Extreme Programming Perspectives.* Addison-Wesley; pp. 355–362.

Humphrey, W. 2002. *Winning with Software.* Boston: Addison-Wesley.

Humphrey, W. 2000. *Introduction to Team Software Process.* Boston: Addison-Wesley.

Humphrey, W. 1997. *Managing Technical People.* Reading, MA: Addison-Wesley.

Humphrey, W. 1997. *Introduction to the Personal Software Process.* Reading, MA: Addison-Wesley.

Humphrey, W. 1995. *A Discipline for Software Engineering: The Complete PSP Book.* Reading, MA: Addison-Wesley

Humphrey, W. 1989. *Managing the Software Process.* Reading, MA: Addison-Wesley.

Intelliware Development, Inc. October 25, 2002. "XP Metrics" presentation.

Jacobson, I., G. Booch, and J. Rumbaugh. 1999. *The Unified Software Development Process.* Reading, MA: Addison-Wesley.

Juran, J.M. 1988. *Juran on Planning for Quality.* New York: MacMillan.

Kaplan, R., and D. Norton. 1996. *The Balanced Scorecard: Translating Strategy into Action.* Boston: Harvard Business School Press.

Kruchten, P. 2002. Presentation to the Iterative, Adaptive, and Agile Processes Workshop at ICSE, May 25, 2002.

Kruchten, P. December 2001. "Agility with the RUP," *Cutter IT Journal*; pp. 27–33; www.therationaledge.com/content/jan_02.

Kruchten, P. 1999. *The Rational Unified Process (2nd Ed. 2001).* Reading, MA: Addison-Wesley.

Li, W., and M. Alshayeb. 2001. "An Empirical Study of Extreme Programming Process," *Proceedings, 17th Intl. COCOMO/Software Cost Modeling Forum.* USC-CSE.

Lim, W. 1998. *Managing Software Reuse.* Prentice-Hall.

McBreen, P. 2003. *Questioning Extreme Programming.* Boston: Addison-Wesley.

McGarry, J., and R. Charette. 2003. "Systemic Analysis of Assessment Results from DoD Software-Intensive System Acquisitions," Tri-Service Assessment Initiative Report, Office of the Under Secretary of Defense (Acquisition, Technology, Logistics).

McGibbon, T. 1996. "Software Reliability Data Summary," Data Analysis Center for Software Technical Report.

Malan, R., and K. Wentzel. April 1993. "Economics of Reuse Revisited," HP Labs Technical Report HPL-93-31.

Manzo, J. March 2003. "Agile Development Methods, the Myths, and the Reality: A User Perspective," *Proceedings, USC-CSE Agile Methods Workshop.* http://sunset.usc.edu/events/past.

Manzo, J. October 2002. "Odyssey and Other Code Science Success Stories," *CrossTalk*, Hill Air Force Base, Utah: U.S. Air Force Software Technology Support Center; pp. 19–21, 30.

Marenzano, J. 1995. "System Architecture Validation Review Findings," in D. Garlan, ed., *ICSE Architecture Workshop Proceedings*. Pittsburgh: Carnegie-Mellon University.

Maurer, R., and S. Martel. April 8, 2002. "Agile Software Development: An Industrial Case Study," CeBASE Agile Methods e-Workshop No. 1. http://fc-md.umd.edu/projects/Agile/Maurer.htm.

Musson, R. September 2002. "How the TSP Impacts the Top Line," *CrossTalk*, Hill Air Force Base, Utah: U.S. Air Force Software Technology Support Center; pp. 9–11.

Nawrocki, J., and Wojciechowski. 2001. "Experimental Evaluation of Pair Programming," *Proceedings, ESCOM 2001*; pp. 269-276.

Nosek, J. March 1998. "The Case for Collaborative Programming," *Communications of the ACM*; pp. 105–108.

Palmer, S., and J. Felsing. 2002. *A Practical Guide to Feature-Driven Development (The Coad Series)*. Upper Saddle River, NJ: Prentice Hall.

Parnas, D. March 1979. "Designing Software for Ease of Extension and Contraction," *IEEE Transactions on Software Engineering*; pp. 128–137.

Paulk, M. October 2002. "Agile Methodologies and Process Discipline," *CrossTalk*. Hill Air Force Base, Utah: U.S. Air Force Software Technology Support Center; pp. 15–18.

Paulk, M., and M. Chrissis. January 2002. "The 2001 High Maturity Workshop," CMU-SEI-2-1-SR-014, Pittsburgh: Software Engineering Institute/Carnegie-Mellon University.

Paulk, M., et al. February 1993. *Capability Maturity Model for Software, Version 1.1* (CMU/SEI-93-TR-24, ADA263403). Pittsburgh: Software Engineering Institute/Carnegie-Mellon University.

Paulk M., et al. August 1991. *Capability Maturity Model for Software*. Pittsburgh: Software Engineering Institute/Carnegie-Mellon University. CMU/SEI-91-TR-24, DTIC Number ADA240603.

Pavlik, R., and C. Riall. February 2002. "Integrating PSP, TSP, and Six Sigma at Honeywell," *Proceedings, SEPG 2002*. Pittsburgh: Software Engineering Institute/Carnegie-Mellon University.

Peters, T. 1991. *Thriving on Chaos*. New York: HarperCollins.

Poulin, J. 1997. *Measuring Software Reuse*. Reading, MA: Addison-Wesley.

Prowell, S., et al. 1999. *Cleanroom Software Engineering: Technology and Process*. Reading, MA: Addison-Wesley.

Rechtin, E. 1991. *Systems Architecting*. Prentice-Hall.

Reifer, D. 2002. "How to Get the Most Out of Extreme Programming/Agile Methods," *Proceedings, XP/Agile Universe 2002.* Springer; pp. 185–196.

Reifer, D. 1997. *Practical Software Reuse.* John Wiley and Sons.

Rostaher, M., and M. Hericko. 2002. "Tracking Test-First Pair Programming—An Experiment," *Proceedings, XP/Agile Universe 2002.* Springer; pp. 174–184.

Royce, W.E. 1998. *Software Project Management: A Unified Framework.* Reading, MA: Addison-Wesley.

Schwaber, K. 1995. "Scrum Development Process," OOPSLA'95. Workshop on Business Object Design and Implementation. New York: Springer-Verlag.

Schwaber, K., and M. Beedle. 2002. *Agile Software Development with Scrum.* Upper Saddle River, NJ: Prentice-Hall; p. 20.

Sheard, S. July 2003. "The Life Cycle of a Silver Bullet," *CrossTalk.* Hill Air Force Base, Utah: U.S. Air Force Software Technology Support Center.

Shull, F. et al. June 2002. "What We Have Learned about Fighting Defects," *Proceedings, Metrics 2002.* IEEE; pp. 249–258.

Sliwa, C. March 18, 2002. "Users Warm Up to Agile Programming," *Computerworld*; p. 8.

Stapleton, J. 2003. *DSDM: Business Focused Development (2nd Ed.).* Boston: Addison-Wesley.

Stapleton, J. 1997. *DSDM, Dynamic Systems Development Method: The Method in Practice.* Reading, MA: Addison-Wesley.

Taylor, D. 1997. *Object Technology: A Manager's Guide.* Reading, MA: Addison-Wesley.

Thorp, J. 1998. *The Information Paradox.* McGraw-Hill.

Tucker, A. September-October 2002. "On the Balance between Theory and Practice," *IEEE Software*.

USC-CSE. "MBASE Guidelines" and "MBASE Electronic Process Guide." http://sunset.usc.edu/research/MBASE.

Van Cauwenberghe, P. 2003. "Refactoring or Up-Front Design?" in Marchesi, M. et al., ed. *Extreme Programming Perspectives.* Boston: Addison-Wesley; pp. 191–200.

Van Duersen, A. November 2001. "Customer Involvement in Extreme Programming," *ACM Software Engineering Notes*; pp. 70–73.

Vu, J. March 2000. "Process Improvement in the Boeing Company," *Proceedings, Software Engineering Process Group 2000*, Software Engineering Institute.

Webb, D. June 2000. "Managing Risk with TSP," *CrossTalk.* Hill Air Force Base, Utah: U.S. Air Force Software Technology Support Center.

Webb, D., and W. Humphrey. February 1999. "Using TSP on the Task View Project," Hill Air Force Base, Utah: U.S. Air Force Software Technology Support Center; pp. 3–10.

Weinberg, G. 1971. *The Psychology of Computer Programming.* New York: Van Nostrand-Reinhold.

Williams, L. and R. Kessler. 2002. *Pair Programming Illuminated.* Boston: Addison-Wesley.

Williams, L., R. Kessler, W. Cunningham, and R. Jeffries. August 2000. "Strengthening the Case for Pair Programming," *Software*; pp. 19–25.

Womack, J., D. Jones, D. Roos. 1991. *The Machine That Changed the World: The Story of Lean Production.* New York: HarperCollins.

www.adaptivesd.com

www.dsdm.org

www.itabhi.com

www.rational.com

www.sei.cmu.edu

XP Universe and First Agile Universe Conference 2002 Proceedings. August 2002. Don Wells and Laurie Williams, editors. LNCS 2418, Lecture Notes in Computer Science Series, G. Goos, et al., eds. Heidelberg/New York: Springer.

Yourdon, E. 1999. *Death March: The Complete Software Developer's Guide to Surviving "Mission Impossible" Projects.* Upper Saddle River, NJ: Prentice-Hall PTR.

Index

A

Acceptance tests, 74, 78
A-Churn risks, 102, 108, 110, 112, 116, 119, 122, 124, 127, 131, 133, 136, 138, 145
Ada, 90–94
Advanced Automation System (FAA), 23, 46
Agent-based planning systems, 104–106
Agile Alliance, 16
Agile Manifesto
  communication and, 35
  described, 2–3, 16–17, 195–196
  responsiveness to change and, 26–27
Agile methods. *See also* Agile Manifesto; Agility
  application characteristics and, 25, 27–37
  characteristics of, 17–18
  described, 2–7
  examples of, 21–22, 59–89
  finding middle ground and, 22–24
  five critical factors associated with, 54–57
  high-change environments and, 29–31
  history of, 18
  key concepts for, 18–19
  management characteristics and, 25, 31–37
  misconceptions about, 53–54
  personnel characteristics and, 25, 44–50
  primary goals of, 26–31
  purist interpretations and, 8
  revolutionary character of, 50
  risk-based methods and, 99–146
  studies of, 225–233
  technical characteristics and, 25, 37–44
  wide adoption of, 4

AgilePlus, 146, 233
Agile Software Development (Cockburn), 153–155
Agile Software Development Ecosystems (Highsmith), 153
Agility. *See also* Agile Manifesto; Agile methods
  discipline and, balancing, 99–146, 156–158
  finding middle ground and, 22–24
  need for, in future applications, 151
  role of, 1–24
  use of the term, 5
Air Force (United States), 15, 90–95, 188
Anchor point milestones, 101, 104, 117, 205–209
Applications, characteristics of, 25, 27–37
Architecture, 13, 15
  BDUF and, 42
  "breakers," 40, 86
  case studies and, 85–86, 89, 91, 93–95
  day-in-the-life examples and, 77
  described, 13
  determining the optimum quantity of, 220–225
  reduced development cycle time and, 41–42
  risk-based methods and, 107, 115, 141–143
  robust, 77
  SAIV process model and, 214
  traditional development and, 2
  wasted resources and, 42
Army (United States), 28–29, 106. *See also* Future Combat Systems (United States Army)
A-Scale risks, 102, 110, 115, 119, 122, 124, 127, 131, 133, 136, 138, 145
ASD (Adaptive Software Development), 21, 166, 170–171, 194

Barry, Rich, and friends.